THE MOST UNUSUAL ~~AND GREAT~~ STORIES
OF BASEBALL HISTORY!

Here is a unique collection of fascinating, little-known tales of the heroes, the scoundrels, the fights, the feuds, the unbeatable records, the incredible errors, the tragedy and the comedy of America's favorite game.

Learn the truth about the last days of Babe Ruth.

Tickle your funny bone with the hilarious story of the only man on an all-girl baseball team.

Read the amazing story of the pro ballplayer who became the President of the United States.

Chuckle at the tale of the only player in history who ever stole first base.

Learn the little-known facts about the famous Black Sox scandal.

Thrill to the inspiring story of the deaf-mute who went on to become one of the game's greatest players.

BASEBALL'S UNFORGETTABLES

BASEBALL'S UNFORGETTABLES
BY MAC DAVIS

BANTAM PATHFINDER EDITIONS
TORONTO/NEW YORK/LONDON

RLI: $\dfrac{\text{VLM } 6.0}{\text{IL } 7\text{–}12}$

BASEBALL'S UNFORGETTABLES
A Bantam Pathfinder Book | published March 1966

2nd printing ..... April 1966	6th printing ...... April 1970
3rd printing ..... March 1967	7th printing .... January 1971
4th printing ...... May 1969	8th printing .. November 1971
5th printing ...... April 1970	9th printing .. September 1972

10th printing .... September 1972
11th printing

Library of Congress Catalog Card Number: 66-14717

Published simultaneously in the United States and Canada

Bantam Books are published by Bantam Books, Inc. Its trade-
mark, consisting of the words "Bantam Books" and the por-
trayal of a bantam, is registered in the United States Patent
Office and in other countries. Marca Registrada. Bantam
Books, Inc., 666 Fifth Avenue, New York, New York 10019.

PRINTED IN THE UNITED STATES OF AMERICA

BASEBALL'S UNFORGETTABLES

MY LICK AT BAT

This book needs an introduction about as much as Mickey Mantle or Willie Mays needs a lesson on how to play baseball. For this is one sports book that will speak for itself.

However, since I am its author, let me guide you to your grandstand seat with just a few brief words of welcome.

No chapter in the history of American sports is stranger, more incredible, or more glorious than that composed by the men of the diamond. The romance of baseball flows from generation to generation enriching memory with treasures of fact, legend, lore, and myth.

In a labor of love, I have put together a unique collection of the most unusual and offbeat stories in baseball that reveal all the glamour, color, thrills, drama, mystery, tragedy, and humor of America's favorite game. This book is not a history of baseball, nor is it intended to be such. But across its pages march in kaleidoscopic review all the unforgettable people from the wonderful world of baseball, since the game began. In this parade of stories one may well discover the folklore of baseball.

No matter how well informed you may be in the lore and legends of baseball, you will find things in here that you've never known before.

So be you a dyed-in-the-wool baseball fan, a casual spectator, or even a stranger to the diamond game, in this book you will discover much that will amaze, shock, surprise, and intrigue you, and beyond doubt convince all that, in baseball, truth is often far stranger than fiction.

It is hoped that you will find *Baseball's Unforgettables* unforgettable reading.

MAC DAVIS

7

THE CLOSEST BATTING DUEL

In 1910 there was a duel fought between two players for a major-league batting championship which became so heated that even other players in the league took sides. The finale not only aroused angry charges of skulduggery, but even resulted in the expulsion of a major-league manager and a player-coach from big-league baseball.

The two Hall of Famers who slugged it out for that American League bat title were second basemen Napoleon Lajoie, the most graceful player there ever was, and Ty Cobb, the greatest hitter and all-around player of all time. All season long, those two baseball greats dueled for the bat crown, but neither could pull away from the other.

On the last day of the season, Lajoie, who was then with the Cleveland Indians, played a double-header against the St. Louis Browns. In the two games, he went to bat nine times, and he made eight hits. Oddly, four of those hits were bunts to the Browns' third baseman. He finished the season with a .384 batting average. But Ty Cobb also finished the season with a .384 batting mark. However, he refused to share the American League batting title with Napoleon Lajoie. He charged that the St. Louis manager, Jack O'Connor, and player-coach Harry Howell had connived to help Lajoie get away with four safe bunts to the Browns' rookie third baseman, so as to fatten up his batting average and help him wind up that season with the highest batting mark in the league. After an investigation was made by the president of the league, the St. Louis manager and his player-coach were kicked out of the big leagues, and Ty Cobb was publicly declared to be the official winner of the American League championship for 1910—with a final batting mark of .3848, while Lajoie was given second place with a final mark of .3841.

Thus, by the slim margin of only seven tenths of a point, the most stirring, the closest, and the most controversial duel ever fought for a major-league championship ended.

HE WAS GOD'S OUTFIELDER

William Ashley Sunday (Billy Sunday) heard the voice of God one day and became God's outfielder.

Reared in an orphan asylum, he was plucked off the Iowa sand lots to play in the big leagues for the old Chicago White Stockings. On May 22, 1883, he made his major-league debut and quickly set a baseball record that still stands. He struck out the first fourteen times he came to bat.

Nevertheless, Billy Sunday gained fame as a big-league outfielder. He was the first major-league player to circle the bases in less than twelve seconds.

Although he became one of the greatest and highest paid major-league stars of his time, he took his fame and fortune lightly. He was the wildest, gayest, and most notorious playboy in the baseball world.

One night during his ninth season in the majors, as Billy Sunday was sauntering out of a saloon, he suddenly heard his mother's favorite song: "Where Is My Wandering Boy Tonight?" It was being sung in a nearby rescue mission church. He entered and suddenly "got religion."

He told his gay companions of the night: "I heard the Lord ask me to play ball for Him, so I signed up! Boys, I'm finished with baseball and this wild life, for I've seen the Light! I'm going into the service of God!"

No one believed him, but he suddenly quit the major leagues. He began working for the Young Men's Christian Association—for only eighty-three dollars a month.

Soon after, he became an evangelist whose style of preaching was as exuberant as his ballplaying had been. In the fury of his preaching to sinners, he would leap on chairs, fling himself on the floor in imitation of a ballplayer sliding to base, and he would spar and box with a heckler if need be.

"I'm God's outfielder!" he shouted, and Billy Sunday became the world's most famous evangelist for almost forty-three years.

When his health began to fail, he said to his friends: "I'm on third base waiting to go on home." In 1935 Billy Sunday, God's outfielder, "went home."

THE FIRST WONDER BATTER

To hit .400 is a feat, rare enough in itself, but for a ballplayer to hit .400 three times is a remarkable achievement. Jesse Burkett, the first great batting king in the history of the major leagues, did it.

Jesse Burkett, who stood no more than five-eight and weighed only 160 pounds, was a pitcher before the turn of the century.

In the season of 1890, he was a pitcher with the New York Nationals. But he was a failure. He lost too often. His big-league days seemed to be over. Then, in his darkest moment, someone casually remarked that Jesse Burkett had more of a chance to stick in the big leagues as a fly-chaser than as a pitcher. Like a drowning man, the hopeless pitcher grabbed at the straw. Then and there, he decided to abandon his pitching and become an outfielder. On that curious switch, baseball history was made.

Five years later, Jesse Burkett, the pitching failure, was an outfielder with the Cleveland baseball club. He finished the 1895 season with an astonishing batting average of .423!

The following season, again Jesse Burkett wielded a potent bat, and completed that pennant campaign with a .410 batting average. Three years later, he batted himself into Hall of Fame immortality, because for the third time, he batted over the .400 mark. His final batting average for that season was .402.

Thus, Jesse Burkett, who was a failure as a big-league pitcher, curiously, became the first player in the history of baseball to bat over .400—three times.

THE GREATEST MANAGER THERE EVER WAS

On May 16, 1894, John J. McGraw, pasty-faced little Irishman who was the star third baseman for the Baltimore Orioles of old, precipitated a violent and costly fist fight. On that afternoon, the legendary Orioles were playing the Boston club in their Beantown ball park.

The game wasn't many innings old before firebrand McGraw became involved in several squabbles, which stirred up the hostile home-town crowd into an angry frenzy. But, though little, McGraw wasn't a man to calm and soothe a baseball mob. So before long, he picked a fist fight with Boston's popular first baseman, Tommy "Foghorn" Tucker. In the flash of a wild moment, it turned into the fiercest free-for-all and costliest fist fight in baseball history!

For while pugnacious McGraw and his teammates were throwing punches at the Boston players, some of the more exuberant fans decided to add to the excitement on the ball field. They set the bleachers on fire!

That fire spread and burned down the ball park. But even more unbelievable, that fire spread far beyond the ruined ball park, and burned down 170 buildings. It caused property damage running into millions of dollars!

In the middle of the 1902 baseball season, the runty John McGraw was appointed the new manager of the New York Giants. He remained their skipper for thirty years.

John McGraw, who became a swashbuckling and universally known major-league manager, was nicknamed "The Little Napoleon" of baseball. In the dugout, he sat in a specially built raised seat that looked like a throne, playing the supreme dictator. He ruled his Giant players with an iron hand. He made all the decisions and used his players as his whims dictated. But no manager ever molded more players for Hall of Fame immortality than John McGraw.

Only McGraw piloted a team to win seventeen

games in a row, on the road. Only McGraw managed a team to win twenty-six games in a row, at home, in a single season.

Manager McGraw enriched big-league baseball with many innovations. He was the first pilot to manage from the bench, the first to use a relief pitcher, and the first to use a player strictly for the sole duty of pinch-hitter. When little McGraw was on the big-league scene, the baseball world "jumped" with excitement, turmoil, and controversy. Almost everything he did on and off a ball field made headlines. He became a legend during his lifetime, as he wound up with ten pennants for his everlasting fame.

On June 2, 1932, the Giants lost a close game. Back in the locker room, manager McGraw berated his players harshly. All took it in silence, for never had a player dared talk back to skipper McGraw, the toughest loser in baseball. But that day was different from all the rest. For suddenly, the star third baseman Freddie Lindstrom, the youngest player on the team, angrily exploded and snapped back at McGraw: "Go ahead and call us all the names you want—for you're the Little Napoleon. But as for me, I'm sick and tired of your insults!"

For a shocked moment, manager McGraw just stood there in silence, looking at his brash third baseman. Then he shrugged his shoulders and, without a word, walked out of the dressing room. All the players realized something was wrong, and that something shocking would soon happen. It did, the very next day. For on June 3, 1932, came the unbelievable headline news that manager McGraw was too sick and too weary to go on as the pilot of the Giants. He had turned over the management of the team to his famous first baseman, Bill Terry, the last National League player to hit .400!

After thirty consecutive years at the Giants' helm, John McGraw had quit as a big-league manager. It was the end of the longest reign a major-league skipper ever had. Two years later, he died.

LITTLE BOBBY WAS FIRST WITH FOUR

There is no longer anything unusual about a major-league player who hits a home run. Once the immortal Stan Musial belted five home runs in a single day, during a double-header. Once Roger Maris, a .260-batter, hit sixty-one homers in a single season. And the legendary Babe Ruth socked a fantastic total of 730* home runs during his fabulous career in the big leagues.

But on the afternoon of May 30, 1894, Bobby Lowe performed a feat of home-run slugging which to this day has not been topped, and most likely won't ever be as long as men hit homers for major-league glory.

---

* Babe Ruth hit 714 home runs during the regular season (life-time); fifteen in World Series competition and one in an All-Star Game.

Bobby Lowe was a strange swatsmith for the most unforgettable homer feat in baseball history. For he stood only sixty-eight inches tall, and weighed barely 140 pounds. In the eighteen seasons he played in the majors, he was just another second baseman and hardly ever better than a .200-hitter.

On that Memorial Day, his team played a double-header against the Cincinnati Reds. In the first game, Bobby Lowe, lead-off man for the Boston club, went to bat four times, and—most usual for him—he failed to get even a single hit.

Dejected, he went out and stuffed himself with a huge fish dinner before the start of the afternoon game.

When the game began, for his first time at bat in that contest, Bobby Lowe was an easy out. The large fish meal he had eaten bothered him. In the third inning, when he came to bat again, he was extremely angry. So he belted the first pitch hurled at him, for a home run. It touched off so vigorous a batting rally that, before that inning was over, Bobby Lowe came to bat for a second time. To the amazement of the six thousand spectators in the ball park, he belted another homer, his second in a row.

In the fifth inning, when little Bobby Lowe came to bat again, once more he socked a home run, his third in succession. And the very next time he came to bat, again he belted a homer, his fourth homer in a row! The crowd went wild. Coins tossed netted him nearly five hundred dollars.

In the eighth inning, when he came to bat for his last time, all he could do was hit a puny single.

For a long time after, superstitious Bobby Lowe returned to the restaurant, and stuffed himself with the same large fish dinner he had eaten on that historic day when he had hit four consecutive home runs in a nine-inning game. But he still went hitless. Eventually, he became so disgusted by his failure that he gave up entirely eating fish forever.

Willie Mays' first toy was a baseball. At the age of three, the son and grandson of professional ballplayers was given a baseball glove, and eleven years later the boy was playing semi-pro ball with grown men.

On his twentieth birthday, in May of 1951, Willie came to the major leagues to play center fielder for the former New York Giants. Curiously, he was neither anxious nor happy to begin playing in the big leagues. He had only 116 games behind him in organized baseball and had been content starring in the minors for the Minneapolis Millers. But he had a fantastic batting average of .477.

"You've made a mistake bringing me up here," Willie told the hard-boiled Leo Durocher, who was then manager of the Giants. "You don't want me on your team. I'm not good enough yet."

"Willie, we need you to win the pennant," Durocher said.

In his first game, Willie went to bat five times and failed to hit. Moreover, while chasing a fly ball in the outfield, he knocked over a teammate. In the beginning, twelve times Willie went to bat without hitting. Finally, he made his first hit in the majors. It was a home run. But that was his only safety in twenty-six times at bat.

As the days of that season passed, Willie lifted his puny .038 batting average to over .300 and played so magnificently that he sparked and inspired his teammates to the most miraculous pennant triumph in baseball history.

But the spirit behind the Giants' pennant miracle of 1951 was gone from the majors for the next two years. Willie was in the service of his country with the United States Army. When he returned to the big leagues in 1954 to play in his first full season, he blazed across the baseball scene like a streaking comet. Ever bubbling with laughter and happy talk, the "Say Hey, Kid" as he was nicknamed, belted 41 homers, drove in 110 runs, and batted .345 to win the National League batting championship. Moreover, again he sparked the Giants to a pennant, and a World Series championship. That unforgettable year, Willie also won the "Most Valuable Player" award for his first time.

As he became one of the greatest center fielders of all time, the record books began to bulge with his amazing feats. He became the first player in history to hit 30 homers and steal 30 bases in a single season. He also became the first player ever to hit 200 home runs and steal 200 bases.

In his first two thousand major league games, he collected 2,382 hits, 505 home runs, 1,000 extra-base hits, and more than 300 stolen bases. For nine seasons in a row, he batted in 100 or more runs, and for twelve consecutive seasons, he scored 100 or more runs. Willie's consistency, durability, and performance over the years not only made him the most famous and glamorous star in the majors, but also the highest-paid baseball player of all time.

In 1965, the baseball world expected the "Say Hey, Kid" to slow down on the glory road. He was thirty-four. But he starred again in a fantastic season for his everlasting fame. He lashed out 178 hits for a .317 batting average, he scored 118 runs, batted in 112 and he belted 52 home runs. It was a glorious season in which he broke records of his own, and tied many more.

When that unforgettable season ended, Willie Mays won the "Most Valuable Player" award again. And just by winning that coveted baseball honor, he achieved another unique record for his fame as a diamond immortal. No other baseball-great in major-league history ever won two MVP awards eleven years apart.

THE BOSS DOESN'T ALWAYS KNOW BEST

In the long history of the All-Star classic in which the greatest players in the National League play the most famous stars in the American League, there have been many heroes to glamorize the midsummer contest for major-league glory. But pitcher Carl Hubbell became the All-Star hero of the ages when, in the 1934 game, he faced one of the toughest assignments ever inflicted on a big-league hurler.

He almost lost his unique glory, however, because he was doubtful of his greatness, too cautious, and too willing to follow a manager's advice on how to pitch.

For the 1934 All-Star game, Bill Terry was the pilot of the National League All-Star team by virtue of his winning the pennant and the World Series with his New York Giants the previous season.

Manager Bill Terry, a Hall of Fame first baseman, as well as a .400 hitter during his playing days, was a master of detail and sound strategy. He was most anxious to win that All-Star game. So he collected all his National League stars for a secret clubhouse talk before game time, to give them his valued advice on how to play and win that classic.

Terry gave special instructions to his starting pitcher, Carl Hubbell, who had helped him win a pennant and World Series championship. He advised that great Giant pitcher to pitch most cautiously to the formidable array of sluggers in the American League line-up, featuring such immortals as Babe Ruth, greatest home-run slugger of all time, Jimmy Foxx, the second greatest home-run slugger in history, mighty Lou Gehrig, Al Simmons, and Joe Cronin. In their time, those five Hall of Fame immortals accounted for more than two thousand home runs.

That All-Star game began, and Carl Hubbell, following his manager's advice, started pitching most cautiously, even a little fearfully. The first batter to face him quickly lined out a single. Overcautious, Carl Hubbell walked the next batter. Now up to bat came mighty Babe Ruth, the scourge of all pitchers. If ever a major-league hurler was on the spot, Carl Hubbell was that man. Now, he was just one pitch away from becoming the biggest flop in All-Star history!

However, his catcher stopped playing, walked out to the mound, spat into the dirt to show his disgust, and snarled at the pitcher: "Look, Hub, forget all that junk Bill Terry told you about pitching carefully. Just throw that screw ball of yours at all them bums, and we'll get them out in a hurry!"

So, Carl Hubbell ignored his manager's advice to pitch cautiously, and he began to throw his famed screw ball at the batters. He struck out Babe Ruth on three pitched balls. Up to bat came Lou Gehrig, and Hubbell struck him out on three pitched balls. Then up to bat came the murderous Jimmy Foxx, and Hubbell struck him out, too.

The vast crowd in the stands sat stunned as that first inning ended, not believing what it had seen. For he had struck out Ruth, Gehrig, and Foxx, the three mightiest home-run sluggers in history, with only ten pitches! But Carl Hubbell wasn't yet done with All-Star glory. In the second inning, he struck out Joe Cronin, the first batter to face him. Then he struck out mighty Al Simmons, and then he struck out the sixth batter in a row. It was an exhibition of All-Star pitching that hasn't been equaled since.

Not all big-league ballplayers stick only to baseball—some become "clothes horses" and Beau Brummells of distinction.

The biggest Beau Brummell of them all was the legendary Michael "King" Kelly. He was the first "fashion plate" in baseball history.

King Kelly, who was paid big money when game admission was fifty cents, was a fantastic big-league ballplayer. During his eighteen seasons in the majors, he was a great center fielder, a catcher, pitcher, played first, second, and third base, and shortstop, too! One of baseball's greatest sluggers, King Kelly was also the most daring base-stealer of his time. He made the cry of his

21

fans: "Slide, Kelly, Slide!" a byword of the game. One of the quickest thinking and trickiest ballplayers of all time, he is said to have "written" many of baseball's rules.

He was the first ballplayer to be followed on the streets by worshiping admirers and autograph hounds. When he started with the old Boston club, his fans gave him two white horses and a gold-trimmed carriage, so he could ride to the ball park in royal style. Many were the times when King Kelly's carriage was so mobbed by admiring fans that the horses were unhitched, and willing hands pulled King Kelly's carriage through the streets, as crowds cheered him, and tossed flowers in his path.

King Kelly was not only a ballplayer for the record book, but a character for the story book.

American billboards featured the handsome, happy-go-lucky Irishman as the country's best-dressed man. Wearing the finest-tailored clothes and the most current styles, he was begged by clothing manufacturers to wear their garments to give them distinction, and they paid him high fees to model the latest fashions.

Even the Continent praised his style and dash in dress, and all Europe acclaimed him as the best-dressed man in the world.

His zest for high and gay living, however, finally caused his downfall as a baseball great. When he slipped from the sports scene, King Kelly went on the stage to earn the money he needed for his fine clothes. On November 8, 1894, at the age of thirty-seven, King Kelly suddenly passed away, a victim of pneumonia.

THE LONGEST WINNING
STREAK STRETCHED TO NOWHERE

Only one major-league club holds the unique distinction of chalking up the longest winning streak that paid off with a pennant. The Chicago National League club performed that same feat—twice.

In 1880 a Chicago team, piloted by Cap Anson, put together a winning streak of twenty-one straight, to win a pennant. Fifty-five years later, in 1935, another Chicago team again put together an amazing winning streak of twenty-one straight, to win a pennant.

However, the most amazing winning streak in all major-league history was put together by another club, and it began and ended in the month of September. But, strangely enough, it turned out to be a winning streak of empty glory.

In 1916, the New York Giants were piloted by the legendary John J. McGraw. The season before, the Giants had finished in last place, and manager McGraw, always the hardest loser in baseball, was in a frenzy to make sure that such a humiliation wouldn't happen again to a team of his.

He furiously drove his players to their best, as he experimented to create a baseball machine that would grind out victories. Early that season, when the Giants were on the road, they put together a winning streak of seventeen straight. To this day, no major-league club has equaled that streak playing away from its home grounds.

But tough John McGraw wasn't fully satisfied with that all-time winning streak of seventeen straight. So, around midsummer, he nearly ripped his team apart as he discarded such famous players as the immortal pitcher Christy Mathewson, the great second baseman Larry Doyle, the unforgettable first baseman Fred Merkle,

23

and the incomparable outfielder Eddie Roush. Coming into September of that pennant campaign, John McGraw practically had a new team.

On September 7, the Giants beat Brooklyn, that season's strongest contender for the pennant. But no one paid much attention to that victory. The next day, the Giants played Philadelphia in a double-header. The Giant pitcher, Poll Perritt, beat them in the first game, but he became riled in the course of it, because he had been so viciously needled by the rival players that he pleaded with manager McGraw to be permitted to pitch the second game of that afternoon. "Let me beat those bums again!" he begged. So, McGraw assigned him to pitch a game for the second time on that September afternoon. Poll Perritt's answer was a four-hit shutout victory.

The double-header victory that pitcher Perritt chalked up for the Giants on that day fired the team into a winning frenzy. As those September days passed, the Giants continued to win. They won ten straight, pushed it up to fifteen straight, then twenty in a row, and still they continued to win. On they went to twenty-one victories in a row, then twenty-two, up to twenty-three, and on and on went the Giants' winning streak.

On September 30, the Giants played a double-header against the old Boston Braves. The Giants' southpaw Rube Benton pitched the first game and won it by a shutout, to chalk up the Giants' twenty-sixth straight victory. But the team lost the second game, and the most amazing winning streak in all major-league history had come to an end. From September 7 to September 30, the astounding Giants had won twenty-six straight games —to record the longest winning streak in major-league competition!

But it was a winning streak of empty glory. That season the team finished in fourth place!

THREE TIMES A SUCKER

The World Series has not only catapulted unknowns to fame, but also has humiliated many famous players ever to be recalled as classic goats. To each, be it for glory or shame, it happened only once.

Charley Root, a once famous pitcher for the Chicago Cubs, played the fool three times in a World Series.

In 1929, a great Chicago Cub team met the Philadelphia Athletics in the World Series. The famous Charley Root was given the assignment to hurl the opening game for the Cubs. At the time, he was one of the best pitchers in the majors. However, to face him in that opener, the late Connie Mack sent to the mound his aged, washed-up pitcher Howard Ehmke, who had worked only fifty-five innings during the entire season. The Philadelphia players, as well as all the fans at that game, thought it was some grotesque joke that manager Connie Mack was playing. But in that historic game, old Ehmke played the part of the hero, and Charley Root played the part of a goat—because Ehmke produced one of the greatest surprises in World Series history by pitching a winning masterpiece and setting a new classic record in striking out thirteen batters.

In the fourth game of that 1929 World Series, a chastened Charley Root was back on the mound again pitching for the Cubs. When the Philadelphia team went to bat in the seventh inning, the score was 8–0 against it, and Charley Root had given up only two measly hits. Up to bat came the Hall of Fame slugger, Al Simmons, and Charley Root tried to strike him out to preserve his shutout. It was a fatal mistake. Root grooved one, Simmons connected for a home run, and it touched off the most fantastic batting rally in World Series history. Before that inning was over, Charley Root had been shelled off the mound, the Athletics had made ten runs and won the ball game, practically clinching the world championship. Once again, unlucky Charley Root wound up playing the tragic role of a classic goat.

He didn't show up again in a World Series until three years later, when on October 1, 1932, again he found himself on the mound pitching for the Chicago Cubs against the New York Yankees.

It was the third game of that World Series. The fabulous Yankees had won the first two games, and the hostile mob of fifty thousand home-town rooters was in no mood for another defeat.

In the fifth inning, up to bat came the immortal home-run slugger Babe Ruth. The Chicago rooters villified him more than ever, for already he had hit one home run. They pleaded with Charley Root to strike him out.

Defiantly, the "King of Swat" took two strikes, and then, he pointed to the center-field bleachers to show the jeering crowd the exact spot where he would hit a home run. Charley Root hurled the ball, Babe Ruth connected, and the ball sailed into the bleacher stands only inches away from the spot to which he had pointed.

No player in classic history was ever as unfortunate as unlucky Charley Root.

* * *

Alva "Bobo" Holloman's baseball career ended as fast as it began. On May 6, 1953, the rookie pitcher for the St. Louis Browns, made the most unbelievable major-league debut in modern baseball history. In his very first big-league start, he accomplished a feat never achieved by any other freshman hurler. He pitched a no-hit no-run game against the Philadelphia Athletics.

But his fame fizzled out so quickly that even before the end of his first season in the big leagues, Bobo Holloman was back in the minors.

Second baseman William "Duke" Kenworthy's greatest excitement came not on the field but in a letter.

Duke Kenworthy lasted only two seasons in the majors, earning no more than three thousand dollars a year. But on August 28, 1915, while playing second base for Kansas City of the old Federal League, Duke Kenworthy hit his first and only home run of that season. When he went into the locker room to celebrate, he found a telegram waiting for him that shocked him into a numb silence. An uncle in England had died and had willed him one million dollars.

Another story of good fortune is told about William Griffiths. In 1905, he was the first basemen for the Salt Lake City baseball club, then known as "The Rhyolites." As with all bushers, he was yearning for the glorious day when he would find fame and fortune in the big leagues. But he found neither, only because of a pebble.

One afternoon that season, in a late inning of a game being played in the home ball park, a grounder was hit toward first baseman Bill Griffiths. As he set himself to field the ball, it suddenly hit a pebble and sailed over his head.

With disgust, the first baseman walked over to the spot where the ball had taken the bad hop and picked up the loose pebble. But, just as he was about to toss it away, something about it caught his eye. So, he slipped it into his pocket, and went on with the game.

When the game ended, and Bill Griffiths was back in his hotel room, he carefully examined the pebble he had found in the ball park. There was no doubt about it, the little stone was a gold nugget!

That night, secretly, first baseman Griffiths returned to the ball park, and by the light of a lantern, he spent hours searching for pebbles. When he had accumulated a bucketful of stones, he returned to his room. In the morning, he had all the rocks he had found in the ball

park assayed. To his amazement, he discovered that they were worth more than a thousand dollars to the ton.

Bill Griffiths was a bush-league ballplayer, but he was an ingenious business man. So, quietly he set out to contact friends to raise enough cash so he could dicker for the purchase of the ball park. He bought it for a song.

Once that was done, William Griffiths turned the ball park into a mine—to dig for gold. Fittingly, he named his mine, "First Base."

In time, the ball park turned into a gold mine, yielded rich pickings—a fortune in gold. And the former bush-league first baseman, William Griffiths, became a millionaire!

THE PITCHER WITHOUT GUTS

In the 1942 baseball season, when Casey Stengel was the manager of a lagging major-league team then known as the Boston Braves, there came to him a twenty-year-old left-hander in search of big-league pitching fame and fortune. For a while, manager Stengel ignored that rookie southpaw. But one afternoon, when the Braves were playing the Dodgers, Stengel ordered his rookie left-hander to go to the mound and pitch. The pilot was angry that afternoon because the Dodgers had been stealing his team's signs, and he was determined to discourage their thievery. So, his rookie southpaw went to the hill with orders to "dust off" the first Dodger batter he faced. But when the shy, green left-hander failed to do it, manager Stengel stormed out to the mound and lifted him, because he hadn't decked the batter.

When the embarrassed rookie southpaw returned to the dugout, a furious Casey Stengel snapped at him: "Young man, you're through with this team. Pick up your railroad ticket to go back to the minors. You've got no guts!"

Hurt and bitterly disappointed, that humiliated twenty-year-old rookie pitcher who had been accused by his crusty manager of lacking guts quit baseball, joined the Army, and went off to fight in World War II.

Three years later, he returned to the major leagues, bringing with him several battlefield decorations, a presidential citation for bravery under fire, and a set of jittery nerves.

The war-shaken southpaw was a most unimpressive pitcher on his return to the big leagues. But as the seasons passed, he found the road to major-league greatness. Curiously, the older he grew, the greater a pitcher he became. As time went by, he became the greatest southpaw pitcher of all time. He won more games, pitched more innings, struck out more batters, hurled more shutouts, and piled up more twenty-game victory seasons than any other left-hander in major-league history. His name was Warren Spahn.

When southpaw Warren Spahn was forty-three years of age, he was still pitching in the major leagues and had won more than 350 victories. Even more incredible, at that ripe old baseball age, Warren Spahn was the highest-paid pitcher in baseball, earning a salary with the Milwaukee Braves of eighty-five thousand dollars a season.

The one-time timid rookie southpaw, who was fired from his first team on his first day in the majors because a scornful manager thought he lacked guts to pitch in the big leagues, became the first "million-dollar pitcher" in the history of the major leagues. By 1964, Warren Spahn became the first player in history to have earned more than one million dollars in salary just for pitching baseballs in major-league competition.

April 16, opening day of the 1940 season, was a cold, gusty afternoon. Due to a stiff arm, Bobby Feller, the star hurler of the Cleveland Indians, didn't feel too happy with the honor of pitching the baseball opener against the Chicago White Sox. He expected to be knocked out of the box, quickly. The chill wind at his back also disturbed him because it was difficult to make a curve break in a tail wind.

However, from the first inning on, Bob Feller pitched hitless ball, and, when the ninth inning finally came up, he was in front with a 1–0 score. The chilled, slim crowd of fourteen thousand spectators could hardly believe the miracle that was taking place on the ballfield. Never before had a pitcher won an opening day game with a no-hitter. There was no reason to believe that Bobby Feller would become the first to achieve that impossible feat. Never before had he pitched a no-hit game.

But in the ninth inning, he disposed of the last three batters to face him, and he completed his magnificent no-hitter. It was the only time that a baseball opener was brightened by a no-hit performance.

It may never happen again!

* * *

In 1942, when the famous shortstop Lou Boudreau became the manager of the Cleveland Indians, he was only twenty-four-years old. He was the youngest big-league pilot in the history of baseball.

SAY IT AIN'T SO, JOE

As history recorded it, eight players of the pennant-winning Chicago White Sox team were accused of "throwing" the 1919 World Series to the Cincinnati Reds and all were forever exiled from organized baseball. But outfielder Joe Jackson, who had been a shining big-league baseball hero, evoked the greatest pity for his crime.

Although Joe Jackson had come to the majors as a simple, ignorant, illiterate hillbilly, he proved himself to be one of the most gifted ballplayers of all time. Because he had played bush-league ball without shoes, they nicknamed him in the majors "Shoeless Joe" Jackson. But "Shoeless Joe" was no ballplayer to be ridiculed.

In his first full season in the majors, he achieved a feat no other rookie ever matched. For in the 1911 season he hit. 408!

In the eleven seasons he starred in the majors, "Shoeless Joe" batted mostly from .341 to .395 and he was so fantastic an artist with a bat that the immortal Babe Ruth, greatest home-run slugger of all time, publicly admitted that he had copied Joe Jackson's batting style, and Ty Cobb, the greatest ballplayer of all time, publicly proclaimed Joe Jackson the finest natural hitter in the history of the major leagues.

"Shoeless Joe" Jackson also was peerless as an outfielder, and usually he stole around forty bases each season. But, none too bright, the illiterate outfielder fell in with big-city sharpies, and was persuaded to help "throw" the 1919 World Series for a measly one-thousand-dollar payoff. Even though Joe Jackson was involved in that infamous "Black Sox" scandal, he was so great a ballplayer that in that 1919 World Series he made more hits than all the other players, he hit the only home run, and he wound up as the most brilliant star of that World Series.

But on September 28, 1920, he confessed to a Cook County grand jury that he had accepted a bribe to fix the outcome of the World Series the season before, and for it, he was banished from major-league baseball —for life! It was then that an unknown ragged little boy who had worshiped him as a baseball hero accosted him, and pleaded: "Say it ain't so, Joe!" But the disgraced "Shoeless Joe" Jackson hung his head in shame and quickly hurried off into baseball oblivion. From that moment on, baseball became enriched with a memorable expression that was to stay poignant through the ages. "Say it ain't so, Joe" became baseball's most enduring quotation.

Joe McGinnity was a saloonkeeper pitching semiprofessional ball only on weekends for the purpose of advertising his tavern, when he "schemed" his way into the big leagues. While tending his bar, McGinnity studied the famous major-league pitchers of the day and concluded that they all depended on blazing speed. What baseball needed was a new delivery, he decided. So, smart Joe McGinnity developed a unique pitching delivery—a slow underhand pitch. That submarine delivery of his not only got him into the majors and kept him there for eleven glorious seasons, but also made him a baseball immortal.

In his first year in the majors, pitching for the legendary Baltimore Orioles, baseball's first submarine hurler, won twenty-eight games. The season after, he won twenty-seven games, and the season after that, Joe McGinnity won twenty-six.

However, during his third season in the majors, Joe McGinnity suddenly was kicked out of the big leagues because he had lost his temper. On that day in 1901, while pitching, he became enraged at the famous umpire Tom Connolly, he stepped on his toes, spat in his face, and punched him. For that disgraceful exhibition, Joe McGinnity was expelled from the league by the president of the league.

However, so many fans protested Joe McGinnity's exile from the big leagues, and so fierce was the pressure that he be given another chance, that eventually, he was permitted to return to the majors, only after he had paid a stiff fine, and had publicly apologized to the umpire he had abused.

Having done so, Joe McGinnity, the first submarine pitcher in major-league history, came back to win thirty-one games in one season, thirty-five in another, and twenty-seven in still another pennant campaign. In his eleven years in the majors, he won a total of 247 games.

He also wound up in baseball's Hall of Fame.

But the feat that stamped him as the most unforgettable and the greatest underhand pitcher of all time, as well as the "Iron Man" champion of the majors was achieved in August of the 1903 season. He was then with the New York Giants.

On the afternoon of August 1, the Giants played a double-header. Joe McGinnity hurled not only the first game, but also the second game. He not only pitched two complete games, but he won both games of that double-header.

On August 8, again the Giants played a double-header. And once more "Iron Man" McGinnity pitched the first game, as well as the second. Again, he not only pitched two complete games, but he won both ends of that double-header.

On August 31, again the Giants played a double-header. Sure enough, "Iron Man" McGinnity pitched the first game, as well as the complete second game, and amazingly enough, again he won that double-header. Thus, he became unique as a pitcher of the majors. For he is to this day the only three-time pitcher of a double-header in major-league history, and even more unbelievable, he bunched his trio of double-headers not only in the same season, but the same month. Joe McGinnity won all three double-headers he pitched.

TWO HUMILIATIONS FOR THE BABE

There are endless stories in the treasured legend of Babe Ruth, the superman of the home run. But there are two which are rarely told. Both are of unforgettable humiliations suffered by the greatest home-run slugger there ever was.

In August of 1934, the immortal Babe Ruth, then crowding forty, was playing his twenty-first season in the majors. Although he was still slugging homers, he was definitely past his peak. Some of the younger players felt that the weary, aging "King of Swat" wasn't doing the team much good in its pursuit of the pennant. They grumbled at his presence in right field.

When Babe Ruth learned about it, he became furious. He called a players' meeting. He ordered a meeting of his teammates in the clubhouse behind locked doors. All players came, and Babe Ruth read the riot act to his teammates, ending his tirade by daring any player to stand up and voice a complaint to his face.

There was a deadly silence in the room, as most of the players hung their heads in embarrassment. But suddenly, the famous outfielder Ben Chapman stood up, faced the Babe, and said: "It looks like a lot of our guys suddenly developed poor memories. But I haven't, Babe! I said you weren't doing the team much good this season by remaining in the line-up, and now I say it to your face!"

As he said it, Ben Chapman, a noted scrapper in his time, squared off, prepared for anything that might follow. For the mighty "Bambino" was no player to trifle with. Babe Ruth was stunned. Then he shrugged his shoulders, turned to leave the room, and said: "I might have known it would be a bush-leaguer like you to sound off!"

He hardly spoke to his teammates for the rest of that season. He finished it with only twenty-two homers, and a puny .288 batting average. It was his final season as a player for the Yankees.

The following season, he started with the old Boston Braves. But his heart was no longer in baseball. In a game early that season, weary Babe Ruth came to bat against the Hall of Famer Dizzy Dean, the braggart who claimed that he was the world's greatest pitcher. It was the first time the eccentric hurler had faced baseball's greatest home-run hitter. Dizzy Dean offered to bet fifty dollars that the Babe wouldn't hit a homer against him, even if he fed him only fast balls right down the middle.

Annoyed at Dean's impudence, the Babe accepted that wager. Babe tried, but he lost the bet.

The next afternoon, May 25, 1935, in another game, and against another pitcher, Babe rose in all his wrath and fury as a dying home-run king. He slugged three awesome home runs, to increase his big-league total of homers to 714. It was his farewell to glory. The next day, he left the major leagues forever.

HE SAT OUT THE WORLD SERIES

The goal of every major league manager is to win a pennant. Therefore, it's an unwise pilot who does not go into a World Series with his best players. But strange as it may be, once there was a pennant-winning manager who deliberately refused to use his star player in the post-season classic, simply because he held a grudge against him. The manager of that strange story was Donnie Bush. The star player who didn't play was Hazen "Kiki" Cuyler.

In 1927, Donnie Bush, a once-famous big-league shortstop, was the manager of the Pittsburgh Pirates. It was his first season as a major league pilot. In his first season, Donnie Bush astonished the baseball world by piloting the Pirates to a pennant.

That glorious season, manager Bush had a great outfielder starring for the Pirates. He was Kiki Cuyler, who played in the majors for eighteen seasons. He was a fleet-footed outfielder who could run like a man pursued by demons, throw as if his arm were a slingshot and hit around .350! When the Pirates won the pennant in 1927 for manager Bush, Kiki Cuyler, only 25, was already a World Series hero of great renown. For it had been his magnificent playing two seasons earlier that had won the world's baseball championship for the Pirates. Kiki Cuyler was expected to shine brilliantly in the 1927 World Series.

However Cuyler was a superstitious player, and Donnie Bush was a stubborn pilot. Hence, a bitter feud developed between the two men that was to prove costly to the Pirates in that World Series.

Kiki Cuyler always batted number three in the Pirates lineup. Superstitiously, what he feared most was to bat number two. But shortly before the 1927 World Series was to start, manager Bush had juggled his lineup and moved Kiki Cuyler from his number three spot in the batting order to number two.

"Don't do it, skipper!" outfielder Cuyler had pleaded. "Don't put me in that number two spot. It's a jinx for me!"

"Ridiculous!" snorted Bush. "You're hitting over .330 now and it won't make any difference to you. I want you to bat where I put you!"

Kiki Cuyler refused to shift. So, stubborn manager Bush benched him.

Then came the World Series against the New York Yankees, hailed at the time as the greatest team in history. But Pirate manager Donnie Bush wouldn't yield. He not only wanted his star outfielder, Kiki Cuyler, to bat in the number two spot, but, stubbornly, he also wanted him to say he would hit second in the lineup and like it.

Kiki Cuyler was willing to play in that 1927 World Series and even bat number two, but he refused to tell his manager that he would like it. So, manager Donnie Bush stubbornly and foolishly nursed his grudge, and kept the Pirates' star player and best hitter sitting on the bench—all through that World Series!

With the great Kiki Cuyler forced to sit out the Series, the Pittsburgh team went down to a most humiliating defeat—in four straight games!

It was the only time in history when a famous ball-player, unwillingly, sat out an entire World Series—because his manager stubbornly and foolishly held a grudge against him!

Long ago Fred Goldsmith was an obscure pitcher in the newfangled game of baseball. However, he began to attract some attention when he publicly claimed to have discovered a new pitch—a curve ball. He even claimed that his newly invented curve ball would revolutionize the art of pitching.

Fred Goldsmith's discovery was ridiculed as nothing more than an optical illusion. Everyone said it was impossible for a baseball pitcher to throw a curve ball. So, Fred Goldsmith decided to prove to all skeptics that a curve ball was no optical illusion. He arranged for a public demonstration of his newly invented pitch. The date for that pitching performance was August 16, 1870. A huge crowd turned out to see Fred Goldsmith throw curve balls.

A chalk line was drawn along the ground for a distance of forty-five feet. Three poles were staked in a straight line. Pitcher Goldsmith stood at one end, and his catcher at the other. He wound up and threw the baseball. It went to right of the first pole, left of the second pole, and right of the third pole. The crowd gasped with surprise. He actually had pitched a ball that curved. He did it again and again on that historic day until everyone in that huge crowd was convinced that a curve ball was no optical illusion.

Following that startling exhibition, Fred Goldsmith became known as the "daddy of the curve ball." The big-league professional baseball clubs sought his services as a pitcher, and before long, he was pitching for the old Chicago White Stockings of the National League. With his curve-ball pitching, he became a sensational star, and in six seasons of big-league hurling, he won 114 games.

For a long time after his big-league playing days were over, Fred Goldsmith happily and proudly basked in his fame.

But one day, Fred Goldsmith's pride as the "daddy

of the curve ball" was suddenly shattered. Another pitcher named Arthur Cummings popped up on the baseball scene and claimed that he was the true inventor of the curve ball. Many believed him. It created a heated controversy that lasted for many years. When the ruling powers of big-league baseball ignored old Fred Goldsmith as the real "daddy of the curve ball," it broke him up completely. He sorrowed himself into becoming an invalid. To the end of his life he talked of nothing but the injustice that had been done him as a baseball pioneer. He died clutching the age-yellowed newspaper clippings which reported on his demonstration of the first curve ball ever pitched.

As he had prophesied, he had revolutionized the art of pitching.

* * *

In 1905, when the twenty-seven-year-old coal miner Mordecai Brown first began to pitch in the major leagues, baseball followers snickered. As a big leaguer he was something of a freak—he had only three fingers on his right hand.

Yet right-hander "Three-Fingered" Brown pitched in the majors for fifteen years. Despite the handicap of a mutilated pitching hand, he won 239 games, and he twirled himself into baseball's Hall of Fame to become one of the immortals of the pitching game.

THE VANISHED INDIAN

Louis Sockalexis was the first Indian to play in the major leagues. In his time, he was so great a ballplayer that he grew in the popular imagination as a mythical figure. Although he played only three seasons in the majors, he was acclaimed as one of the greatest players in big-league history.

Sockalexis left the Penobscot Indian reservation to become a famous baseball star at Holy Cross College. Six feet tall, 190 pounds heavy, he was as handsome as a man ever was, and graceful and fast as a race horse. Before the turn of the century, he ran a hundred yards under ten seconds. When Sockalexis played one season in the old Knox County League in Maine, his baseball feats were so heroic that he inspired the manager of one of the clubs in that league to write stories for boys and use him as a model for the fictitious character he created, called "Frank Merriwell." For decades, the Frank Merriwell story books delighted and inspired millions of boys.

In 1897, Sockalexis crashed the major leagues. He became an outfielder for the Cleveland Club, then known as "The Spiders." So overwhelming was his playing that the Cleveland team became generally known as the Cleveland Indians.

But the white man's temptations caused the downfall of Sockalexis. For once at a party, his teammates persuaded him to taste his first strong drink. That one drink sealed his fate as a ballplayer. Thereafter, he couldn't stay away from whiskey and, before long, he became a hopeless drunkard.

After only three seasons, Sockalexis drank himself out of the majors. Eventually, he sank deeper into degradation, until he wound up a forsaken and shabby beggar. In time, he drifted back to the Penobscot Indian reservation from whence he had come, and there he lived in despair and oblivion, until December 24, 1913 when he died at only forty-two.

* * *

In 1945, Bert Shepard, a decorated flying hero of World War II, pitched and played first base for the Washington Senators, even though he wore an artificial leg. For he had lost his right leg as a result of an Army plane crash.

That same season, Pete Gray patrolled the outfield for the St. Louis Browns, starred in seventy-seven major-league games, and batted over .200 even though he was a cripple with only one arm.

THE BUNT

Ballplayer Tim Murnane accidentally originated the bunt.

In 1876 Tim Murnane joined the Boston club when the National League was formed. He was an infielder of little renown. At bat, he was mostly a bust.

One afternoon when the Boston club was playing an important game, Tim Murnane came to bat. He was worried that day, because the manager of the team had soured on him for his weak stick-work. He feared that his days as a big leaguer were numbered if his batting average stayed puny.

The enemy pitcher wound up, let go, and as Tim Murnane saw the ball come sailing plateward, by sheer accident, he gave the ball a whack, a feeble tap with his bat. The ball stopped dead in front of the pitcher's box. However, before the enemy hurler could field that ball speedy Tim easily reached first base.

That surprising hit set Tim Murnane to thinking. With his fertile brain, he saw an opportunity to gain his manager's favor and win some measure of respect as a good batter. So he went home, whittled down flat one side of his bat, then in secret, began to practice his new stroke. He became so skilled that he could lay down a bunt in whatever direction he chose. Because of his invention of the bunt, Tim Murnane became famous and unforgettable in the history of big-league baseball. For when the other players saw what pioneer Tim Murnane achieved with his clever bunting, they also took up the bunt as a diamond weapon. Eventually, skilled bunters became valuable batters in the big leagues. Since then many ball games have been won because of timely and well placed bunts.

The bunt gave Tim Murnane an honored place in baseball history, but it also once caused the end of the major-league career of a famous infielder, Sammy Strang.

For several seasons, Sammy Strang played for John McGraw, the manager of the New York Giants. Sammy

Strang achieved wide fame as the most feared bunter of his time.

One day during the 1908 season, the Giants were playing an important game, and in the ninth inning of that contest they needed a run to break a tie score and win the game. Manager McGraw sent Sammy Strang to bat as a pinch-hitter, with a runner on third. His orders were to "bunt in" the winning run.

However, on that day, Sammy Strang wanted to win that game in a more glamorous way than with a puny bunt. So, on the first pitch, he swung at the ball with all his might, connected, and slugged it far into the stands for a home run. The best bunter in the majors was a happy player as he proudly jogged around the bases to complete his game-winning home run. But to his shocked surprise when he returned to the clubhouse, his manager angrily informed him that he had been fined fifty dollars for disobeying his orders to bunt.

When the startled Sammy Strang heard that he told his stern manager that he would never pay that fine, even if he had to quit baseball. When manager John Mc-Graw refused to relent and cancel the fine, the famous bunter Sammy Strang quit the majors.

THE FIRST FAMOUS HOLDOUT

A financial battle is often waged between stubborn holdouts and tightfisted club owners before the start of every major-league baseball season. Most of baseball's greatest players have been holdouts. Baseball's first famous holdout was outfielder Hugh Duffy, who starred for the old Boston club of the National League.

In 1894, Hugh Duffy achieved a batting feat which hasn't been matched to this day. During that season he won the batting championship with an unbelievable mark of .438! It was the highest batting average ever compiled by a big-league player for a single season.

45

Before the start of the 1895 season Hugh Duffy demanded of his club owner a substantial raise in salary. When it was refused, he held out. He remained a stubborn holdout until finally, the tightfisted club owner capitulated, and Hugh Duffy, baseball's first famous holdout won his fight for a raise in salary.

He won a raise of only $12.50 a month!

Surprisingly, Hugh Duffy wound up a loser even though he had been a winner in his holdout battle. To earn his raise, he had agreed to become the captain of the Boston team and assume responsibility for all the baseball paraphernalia to be used by the club. When the season was over, the cost of the lost paraphernalia came out of his salary and amounted to more than the raise he had received for that season.

It was a sad and bitter lesson Hugh Duffy learned for being baseball's first famous holdout.

No holdout was ever rewarded so miserably as the man who had achieved the highest batting average in big-league history.

THE LITTLE MILLER

Miller Huggins was not impressive in size as a diamond genius. He stood only sixty inches tall. He was only mediocre when he started in the big leagues as a second baseman, but so sharp was his baseball brain, that after nine unimpressive seasons as a player he became a big-league player-manager. As the pilot of the St. Louis Cardinals, it was he who discovered and developed the immortal Rogers Hornsby, the Hall of Fame second baseman, and the greatest right-handed hitter of all time.

In 1918, the pint-sized Miller Huggins was hired to manage the New York Yankees, a club of tough, rowdy, irresponsible ball players which had never won a pennant. He was the biggest baseball joke of that time.

His first few years as the Yankees' manager were

miserable enough to break the spirit and heart of the toughest big-league pilot. The players disobeyed him, ignored his orders, the fans ridiculed him, and rival clubs were amused by the seemingly futile attempts of that "diamond midget" to build the Yankees, then the "poor relations" of the American League, into a pennant winner.

Some of his players physically abused him. Once, on a speeding train, an angry player seized him and threatened to throw him out of the window. Another time, his most famous star, the immortal Babe Ruth, invaded his office and almost beat him up.

But unappreciated Miller Huggins continued to manage the Yankees, and within three seasons he molded the club into a pennant winner, as the Yankees captured their very first flag.

Then Miller Huggins went even further than that. Despite the hostility of his players, the ridicule of the baseball world, and even the doubts of his club owner, he built a foundation for the New York Yankees to become the greatest pennant-winning dynasty in baseball history! In the twelve years he managed the Yankees, he piloted them to six pennants! His 1927 team, to this day, is being acclaimed as the greatest baseball team of all time.

In 1929, Miller Huggins' reign as a Yankee manager suddenly came to an end. One afternoon, late that season, before the day's game was over, he left the dugout, and returned to the clubhouse to shower and dress.

"I'm going home because I don't feel well," he told one of his coaches. "See you tomorrow," said the coach. And the little Miller smiled sadly, and softly replied: "I don't think I'll ever be back!"

He never returned to manage the Yankees again. For on September 25, before that 1929 season had finished, little Miller Huggins died. All his players wept for him, for they had learned to respect his genius as a manager.

Miller Huggins, who had piloted the New York Yankees to their very first pennant, left the club a great inheritance. He had instilled in the Yankees the habit of

47

winning. To this day, the Yankees still honor the memory of the little Miller by more pennants than any other team in the history of the major leagues. By 1964, they had won twenty-eight flags.

For thirty-five years, the tiniest and most unappreciated major-league manager in history remained unrecognized and unhonored as a genius of the diamond. But finally he was rewarded for his greatness. In 1964 he was enshrined in baseball's Hall of Fame.

HOT DOG CHRIS

The frankfurter is almost synonymous with the baseball game. Wherever the game is played, the "sausage on bun" can be found. The "hot dog" was introduced to the sports world by a major-league club owner named Chris Von der Ahe. A colorful, bizarre, and eccentric man, Chris Von der Ahe had been an obscure German saloon-keeper in St. Louis when, some years before the end of the nineteenth century, he suddenly and surprisingly found himself to be the new owner of the St. Louis Browns. He knew nothing of baseball, nevertheless he lost no time in making his baseball club the most talked-about team in the major leagues.

For the bulbous-nosed, comical-looking Chris Von der Ahe who sputtered with an amusing heavy German accent, turned his ball park into an astonishing "Coney Island" playground. With big-league baseball, he also gave to the St. Louis fans brass-band music, beautiful girl trumpeters, shoot-the-chute boat slides from a high tower down into an artificial lake, as well as beer gardens, dancing, and even horse racing, at a track across the street from the ball park.

His players traveled from their hotel to the ball park in open carriages pulled by beautiful white horses. Almost always Chris Von der Ahe would lead his team onto the field in parade formation. Even depositing the daily gate receipts became a special ceremony. For, after every game, the cash was carried to the bank in a wheelbarrow, as the club owner marched behind, armed with a loaded rifle, and flanked by two armed guards.

He hired and fired managers with reckless abandon. One season, he had seven different managers to pilot his team. Once, he even undertook to manage his own team, and he led it to an eleventh-place finish in a twelve-club league.

In victory or defeat, Chris Von der Ahe spent with a lavish hand. Often he bought fancy and expensive suits for all his players to wear. In 1888, when his St. Louis Browns won a pennant, the jubilant Chris tossed a celebration party for his players which cost him fifty-thousand dollars. It was the wildest and costliest baseball party ever staged.

His baseball team became his whole life. Atop the grandstand, he built a luxurious apartment for himself. And he had a life-sized statue of himself placed at the entrance to his ball park.

In 1893, he startled the St. Louis baseball fans with another astonishing novelty. He had a local baker cook up for him a new type of white flour roll, with a sausage inside. It was a juicy concoction of a quick meal which Chris Von der Ahe planned to sell for ten cents at the ball games. His novel invention of a frankfurter on a white roll not only caused a furor of delight in the St. Louis ball park, but quickly, its popularity spread to wherever big-league baseball was played. Eventually, the "hot dog" became an institution in the sports world.

Chris Von der Ahe, who introduced the "hot dog" to baseball, had a pathetic finish as a major-league club owner. He lost his money, his ball park burned down, and he nearly went out of his mind because of his grief. Swamped by lawsuits, deserted by his friends, and betrayed by the other major-league club owners, he was forced to sell his St. Louis Browns for a pittance. He ended his final years on earth in dire poverty. He died a broken-hearted man. When he passed from this world, his last and only wish was granted him: his life-sized statue was placed as a monument over his grave.

A LEFT-HANDED DENTIST WHO WENT RIGHT

More than half a century ago, an obscure, poverty-pinched dentist sadly arrived at the conclusion that there was no future for a southpaw tooth-yanker. So, he turned to professional baseball to eke out a living. On May 10, 1910, the left-handed dentist broke into organized baseball with the Kankakee Club of the old Northern Association. Sometimes he was paid and sometimes he wasn't, and for two years he remained a bush-league outfielder. Drab and dreary was his existence in the new trade, but for him, life was now chock-full of laughter. He was a born clown.

Although the reformed dentist had not set the bush-leagues on fire, nevertheless, in 1912, the old Brooklyn Dodgers bought him for five hundred dollars. On September 17, in that season, he reported to the Dodgers' clubhouse, carrying all his worldly possessions in a shabby paper suitcase. His entire fortune of ninety-five dollars was pinned to his underwear.

When he found his way into the locker room, none of the players paid any attention to him. They were too busy shooting dice. Eventually, he was invited into the crap game, and he quickly lost his entire bankroll.

Before he could get over the shock of his misfortune, the dentist-turned-outfielder was jolted by another surprise on his first day in the majors. The Dodger manager walked in, spotted him, and snapped at him: "Ain't you the rookie they bought? Find yourself a uniform. You're starting in center field this afternoon!"

Garbed in an ill-fitting uniform, without having had a warm-up he walked out on that strange ball field to play against the Pittsburgh Pirates and face the league's leading pitcher. But he made his major-league debut a spectacular day. For in five times at bat, he made four hits, walked, and also stole two bases. In the field, he made several sensational catches.

With an amazing beginning like that, that southpaw ex-dentist quickly found the glory road as a major-league player and starred fifteen years in big-league outfields. He enriched his fame as a big-league outfielder by becoming one of baseball's greatest clowns.

After his playing days in the majors, he didn't leave organized baseball, but turned to managing, and for years toiled unsuccessfully as a big-league pilot. Time and time again, he clowned himself out of his job.

However, after many unsuccessful years, in 1949, when he was nearing sixty, he was awarded the most coveted and most exalted position in the arena of baseball. He became the manager of the fabulous New York Yankees. Everyone was startled and amused.

But as time went by, he astonished the baseball world with unbelievable managerial feats. He became the first and only manager in history to pilot a major-league team to five pennants in a row, and five consecutive World Series championships.

In the twelve seasons he managed the Yankees, he became not only the most famous, the highest-paid, and the richest manager in the game, but also the most successful in the history of the big leagues. In that short span, he piloted the Yankees to ten pennants and seven World Series championships.

When he was past seventy, he was fired by the New York club because he had grown too old. But he refused to retire from baseball. When seventy-five, he was still managing in the major leagues, at a salary of eighty-five-thousand dollars a season. Ironically, he was piloting the New York Mets, the worst team in modern baseball history.

The hero of this baseball saga is Charles Dillon Stengel.

THERE IS NO MORE TRAGIC STORY

On the afternoon of May 2, 1939, shortly before the New York Yankees, the world baseball champions, were about to take the field in a game against the Detroit Tigers —their captain, Lou Gehrig, approached Joe McCarthy, the Yankee manager, and told him:

"I guess you'd better put someone else on first base today. I'm no help to your ball club."

The famous pilot shrugged his shoulders, and simply replied: "Whatever you say, Lou!"

Moments before the start of that May 2 afternoon game, captain Lou Gehrig walked up to the umpire-in-chief, and handed him the team's batting order for that day. The ump casually glanced at it then suddenly his eyes widened and his mouth popped open with surprise. For he saw the name of Babe Dahlgren written in on the batting order, to play first base for the Yankees.

"What's up, Lou?" asked the astonished umpire, "aren't you playing first as usual?" But he quickly stopped asking questions, and turned away with a lump in his throat. The famous first baseman Lou Gehrig sadly shook his head. There were tears in his eyes.

The startling news that Gehrig wasn't going to play first base for the Yankees that May 2 afternoon struck the fans in the ball park like a thunderbolt. Quickly the news spread, and before that game was over, the whole baseball world knew that the incredible Lou Gehrig, the famed "Iron Horse" of the big-league diamonds, had snapped his fantastic consecutive playing streak—the most unbelievable baseball record ever achieved by a ballplayer! For, up to that historic May 2 afternoon of 1939, first baseman Lou Gehrig had set an endurance record for playing major-league baseball games that will never be equaled!

It had taken him fifteen consecutive seasons and untold physical hardships to create that baseball record. Lou Gehrig had played first base for the Yankees in

2130 consecutive major-league games!

To keep that consecutive playing streak alive, in game after game, and season after season, the "Iron Horse" had played despite beatings, cracked ribs, chipped bones, broken fingers, broken toes, muscle tears, wrenched shoulders, pulled ligaments, and lumbago attacks. Yet, through it all, for 2130 consecutive games, the amazing Lou Gehrig refused to seize upon a single accident as an excuse to miss a major-league contest.

And what imperishable glory Lou Gehrig also achieved for his fame as a baseball great during the run of that unbelievable playing streak. He not only became one of the finest fielding first baseman of all time, but also one of the greatest hitters in baseball history! There were seasons when he hit .351—.354—.363—.373 —.374—and .379—to compile an astounding lifetime batting average of .340! He also became the first modern player to hit four home runs in a row, in one nine-inning major-league game. Only he slugged as many as twenty-three "grand slam" homers, and he hit a total of 494 home runs in all, and had helped the Yankees win seven pennants!

Finally, on the afternoon of May 2 in 1939, after he had played in 2130 consecutive major-leagues games, first baseman Lou Gehrig took himself out of the Yankee line-up because he had sadly come to the bitter realization that he was no longer of help to his team.

Lou Gehrig never played again for the Yankees, but, in tribute to their great captain, the team went on to win that season, its fourth straight pennant and fourth consecutive World Series championship!

Hardly more than two years later he was dead from an insidious disease at the early age of thirty-eight.

To this day, no Yankee player has worn Gehrig's famed Number 4 on a baseball uniform. Gehrig's locker in the Yankee clubhouse has become a shrine to his memory. And close by the famed Yankee ball park is a street named in his honor—known as Lou Gehrig Plaza.

May 2, 1939—a day that won't ever be forgotten in baseball history!

THE FIRST DUMMY
WAS NO DIAMOND DUMMY

When twenty-seven-year-old William Ellsworth Hoy first appeared in the big leagues, everybody called him "Dummy." They said he couldn't last. He was deaf and dumb. But William Hoy wasted no time showing the baseball world that he not only belonged in the majors, but that he was one of the brainiest players ever seen on a diamond. For fourteen seasons he was one of the great outfielders of his time. He played for Washington, St. Louis, Cincinnati, and Chicago, and was a fly-hawk in the field. Few outfielders ever threw faster to bases, to nip runners trying to stretch hits to the outfield. He was a consistent hitter, and on the base paths he was an elusive diamond thief. He stole 514 bases.

Because he was a deaf-mute, he couldn't hear the umpire's calls when at bat. So, he asked the umpire to raise his right arm to signify a strike. The idea soon became standard procedure for all big-league umpires. To this day, the umpire behind home plate, calling balls and strikes, always raises his hand for a strike call.

"Dummy" Hoy played in 2327 games. He played his last major-league game when he was past forty-two. When he left the majors, he not only departed from the game with the distinction of being the first deaf-mute to play in the big leagues, but also with the fame of being the greatest deaf-mute ballplayer in baseball history. He lived to be a hundred.

Jackie Robinson, born into the poverty of a sharecropper's cabin on a Southern plantation, first gained fame as a sports hero when he was a college student and became an All-America football and basketball player, a track star, and an outstanding boxer.

But when the twenty-eight-year-old came to the major leagues to play for the former Brooklyn Dodgers, he became the most controversial rookie in baseball history. He was a Negro. Never before had a Negro dared to play in the major leagues. But fearlessly, he consented to try to break down the color barrier in the big leagues.

No player in the long history of major-league baseball ever faced a greater challenge. He became the target of every bigot in the land; he was scorned and humiliated at every turn. Regarded as a freak of the big leagues, rival players openly showed their resentment at his presence in the game. Many refused to play against him, and even some of his own teammates snubbed and ignored him. Again and again his life was threatened if he continued to play in the majors.

Jackie Robinson had to be not only as good as the best in the majors, but even better. He was! He became the Rookie of the Year and, in time, the Most Valuable Player in the National League. Also, he became the league's batting champion, the most daring base-stealer in the game, and the most colorful and most exciting performer of his time. He played first base, second base, third base, shortstop, and the outfield for the Dodgers. And wherever he played he was a star at each post.

Jackie Robinson was so inspiring a player, and so contagious was his wizardry, that, in the ten seasons he starred for the Dodgers, he sparked them to six pennants.

It was Jackie Robinson who completely changed the face of major-league baseball. He shattered the color barrier in baseball, forever. He blazed a trail to the big leagues for all players to follow, regardless of race, color, or creed. Only because of him, there are now more than two hundred Negro players starring in the majors.

When Jackie Robinson was past thirty-eight, although he was still commanding a salary of more than fifty thousand dollars a season as a player, he quit the majors to enter the business world, as a highly paid executive. But the baseball world did not forget his historic feats or his greatness as a ballplayer. He became the first Negro to be enshrined in baseball's Hall of Fame as an immortal of the game.

* * *

How long can an umpire last in the big leagues?

In 1905, little Bill Klem, who had never played professional baseball, began umpiring in the major leagues. On his first day, he incurred the displeasure of a bullying and feared manager who warned him: "I'll have your job before this season is over!" But the spunky newcomer retorted to that threat: "If you can take my job away, then I don't want it!"

Nevertheless, from that ominous beginning, spunky Bill Klem went on to become the most famous, most respected, and greatest big-league umpire of all. He earned an immortal niche in baseball history as "The Old Arbitrator" who never called one wrong.

He umpired in the major leagues for a record thirty-seven years.

* * *

Before the turn of the century, when Cliff Carroll was an outfielder in the National League, he never played without his pet monkey close by. During the 1888 season, when the monkey suddenly died, the grief-stricken ballplayer found a strange and unique grave for his animal friend. For his pet monkey was buried near home plate in the Pittsburgh ball park.

58

Spring training evolved to keep big-league players from a wild life off the field. The annual grind is brief; nevertheless it has become an important business for the major-league club owners, running into millions of dollars. A pennant seed well planted during spring training often has blossomed in October into a World Series championship.

The spring training camp began with Adrian Constantine Anson, now in baseball's Hall of Fame.

No man ever played in the big leagues for as long as Cap Anson. He lasted twenty-seven years. Although, in his time, he was a catcher, second baseman, a third baseman, and a shortstop, too, nevertheless, best of all, he was a first baseman, one of the greatest of all time. In the legends of the game he is considered to be "the daddy" of all great first basemen.

Cap Anson also was one of baseball's greatest hitters. He was the first big-league player in history to make three thousand hits. Twice, he hit over .400 and, for his twenty-seven years in the majors, he wound up with a lifetime batting average of .339! Amazingly, he was also the greatest player-manager the big leagues ever had. For, while he played for the old Chicago White Stockings, Cap Anson piloted his club to five pennants.

Player-manager Cap Anson had a tremendous influence on the growth of big-league baseball. His integrity, sobriety, dignity, and personal purity set a standard for big-league ballplayers. Players out of condition would infuriate him. Forced to manage many tough and wild-living men, Cap Anson not only kept them in line with strong words, but sometimes he would beat up some of the tougher players who dared defy his orders, and ignored his training rules. The start of every baseball season was a trying time for Cap Anson. For his players would report to him hog-fat and woefully out of condi-

tion after a winter of loafing. Finally, he reached the limit of his patience.

In 1886, Cap Anson ordered his players to report to him almost two months before the start of that baseball season. When the puzzled players did, he whisked them off to a training camp he had set up in Hot Springs, Arkansas. He ordered them to "boil out" and he put them through daily rigorous training sessions to get them into good physical condition. His players grumbled and squawked during that first spring training grind, but, when that baseball season started, the Chicago players were in such fine playing condition that they breezed into the pennant.

The "crazy stunt" started spring training for all big-league ballplayers.

Cap Anson is now just an old diamond relic stored away in baseball's Hall of Fame with all the other mementos of a glorious baseball past. But all big-league players still make use of the invention he gave to baseball—the spring training camp.

*   *   *

Baseball is an American invention, and for almost a century now, the game has been a national pastime. But curiously, baseball's first salaried player was a London-born Englishman. In 1864, Alfred James Reach became the first athlete in sports history to be paid for playing baseball. He received one thousand dollars for the season to play first base, second base, and the outfield for the Philadelphia club.

He was also the first baseball player to be traded for money.

Bespectacled ball players are no longer berated.

In recent years, "specs" have made a big hit in the major leagues. There are now some fifty players in the majors who wear them. Among the current crop of "four-eyed flashes" are pitchers, catchers, outfielders, and infielders. Even some major-league umpires have been courageous enough to don a pair of eyeglasses.

In the first half century of the majors, the only player who dared appear on a ball field wearing a pair of glasses was a pitcher named William White. Deacon White was regarded as a freak in those big-league days, nevertheless, he lasted ten years, and three times won more than forty games in a single season.

The first modern major-league player to wear them was another pitcher, Lee Henry Meadows who in the seventeen years he hurled in the majors was known as "Specs" Meadows. In 1927, he and his pitching-teammate Carmen Hill paced the Pittsburgh Pirates to the pennant. Both wore eyeglasses.

Back in 1921, George Torporcer made baseball history when he became the first major-league infielder wearing eyeglasses. "Specs" Torporcer lasted eight seasons in the majors, before his eyes dimmed so that even his "cheaters" wouldn't help him to see. He went totally blind.

A weak-eyed player who once scorned eyeglasses was the little outfielder Paul Waner. When he broke into the majors back in the twenties, his eyesight was so poor that when he was at bat, he could hardly see the outfield fences. Nevertheless, in his first twelve seasons in the majors, nearsighted Paul Waner hit from .321 to .373 and became famous and feared as "Big Poison" in the majors.

After some seventeen seasons of groping around, Paul Waner finally was persuaded to don a pair of eyeglasses. Reluctantly, he began to wear them because he still had one more goal to achieve as a baseball great.

On June 18, 1942, Paul Waner belted a safe hit, and made baseball history. It was his three thousandth major-league hit. His specs had helped him become the seventh player in history to achieve three thousand major-league hits.

The "cheaters" helped him to last twenty-two years in the majors, wind up with 3152 safe hits, and end up an immortal in baseball's Hall of Fame.

THE MOST WONDROUS PITCHER OF ALL

In July of 1948 when the pennant-hungry Cleveland Indians brought the seventy-five-inch, gangling, skinny Leroy "Satchel" Paige to the majors as a rookie pitcher, the baseball world took his coming to the big leagues as an amusing gag. He looked like an ancient gnome on stilts. He claimed to be forty. A Board of Health birth record in his native Alabama showed that he was past forty-two. But friends and neighbors who knew him from his impoverished boyhood in a Mobile slum said that his birth certificate was a fake, and that he was closer to fifty. No one ever found out just how old rookie Satch Paige really was.

As a pitcher, he was a legend even before he came to the major leagues. The venerable hurler had been pitching professionally for more than a quarter of a century, and already he had hurled more than three thousand pro games. During his barnstorming around the baseball world, he had faced a host of famous major-league players, in exhibition contests, and he had made most of them look foolish and futile at bat.

On July 9, 1948, when Satch Paige, the oldest rookie in history, made his debut as a major-league pitcher, it was an historic occasion. He was the first Negro to pitch in the American League.

In his first three starts as a rookie pitcher, more than two hundred thousand people came to the ball park to watch the incredible Satch Paige hurl baseballs at big-league batters. His first appearance in a big-league uniform was witnessed by a record crowd of 78,382 spectators. Satch Paige gave them a performance to remember. For he hurled a three-hit masterpiece to blank the Chicago White Sox by a 1–0 score.

Before that season had ended, the oldest rookie in the history of the big leagues won six crucial games for his team, two by shutouts, and saved several more in relief, to help the Indians win the pennant.

Despite his age, the remarkable Satchel Paige appeared in 178 major-league games. But in less than five seasons he was cast adrift because it was believed that he had grown much too old to pitch in the big leagues.

So, "Old Satch" returned to barnstorming. Although he was again only a cow-pasture pitcher, now crowding sixty, nevertheless he was still so fabulous, and so magnetic was his popularity with the public, that he continued to earn more than fifty thousand dollars a year mowing down batters with monotonous regularity. He even pitched a no-hitter.

Leroy "Satchel" Paige was a professional pitcher for more than forty-five consecutive years. He was the only pitcher in history to win more than two thousand professional games. Even when he was past sixty years of age, he was still hurling professionally, to prove that he was the most durable pitcher who ever lived.

ALL HE COULD DO WAS WIN

He was an unknown farm boy of twenty-three when in the summer of 1890 he first popped up in the big leagues to pitch. The Cleveland baseball club had signed him up to pitch in the majors for seventy-five dollars a month.

The first time the big "hayseed" went to the mound to pitch, he was dressed in a patched-up uniform several sizes too small for him. Everyone laughed at him, but it was the last time anybody ever laughed at Denton Tecumseh Young.

For sixteen years, the pitcher with a rubber arm won twenty or more games a season, and five times he won thirty or more games a season. He was the first pitcher in history to hurl three no-hit no-run games, and the only pitcher in history to hurl no-hitters in both major leagues! Once, he pitched twenty-three consecutive innings without allowing a hit, and at another time won a twenty-inning game, without giving up a single walk. In his time, he struck out 2,819 major-league batters. He was no weakling at bat. He made more hits than any other pitcher in history, and scored more runs than any other hurler.

No one pitched in the majors as long, or participated in as many games, as did Cy Young. He lasted in the majors for twenty-two seasons, and he pitched in 906 games. When he was past forty-five, he finally quit the majors, not because he had lost his pitching skill, but only because he had grown too fat to field bunts. He left behind him a record of having won 511 major-league games.

He is still an inspiration to all hurlers in the major leagues. At the conclusion of every baseball season, the "Cy Young Award" goes to the greatest pitcher in the big leagues. It is the highest honor that is bestowed upon a pitcher for his fame and fortune.

A PITCHER'S MASQUERADE

Early this century, the original Kansas Bloomer Girls, the most famous baseball club of girl players baseball has ever known, featured for a time a strong-armed pitcher with long blond curls. That Bloomer Girl pitcher was sensational and, wherever the Kansas Bloomer Girls toured to play pro baseball, huge crowds flocked to the ball park to see that hurler with the long blond curls pitch. Then one day, it was revealed that the sensational strong-armed pitching star of the Kansas Bloomer Girls was a fraud! For that Bloomer Girl pitcher wasn't a girl at all, but a boy in disguise.

The pitcher was fired, but the Bloomer Girls continued to tour the country as a baseball attraction.

The "Bloomer Girl," however, made the big leagues. For nine years, he starred for the Boston Red Sox as a fast-ball pitcher, winning more than 125 games, and for five years more, he starred for the Cleveland Indians as an outfielder.

In the records of major-league baseball, the "Bloomer Girl" is known as "Smokey Joe" Wood.

THE FIRST BASEBALL GAME

On the afternoon of June 19, 1846, at a popular summer resort site known as the Elysian Field, in Hoboken, New Jersey, a championship baseball game was played between two teams—the Knickerbockers and New York Nine. One hundred spectators were there to witness the baseball contest.

The Knickerbockers, the first organized baseball club in existence, was composed of gentlemen high in the social stratum of the time, financiers, doctors, lawyers, and merchants. They lined up for that game with

67

Turney, Tucker, Tryon, Adams, Avery, Brouthers, Anthony, Paulding, and Birney. The players wore caps, well-tailored long trousers, silk shirts with cravats.

The New York Nine was composed of players from a lower social stratum. They were humble mechanics, clerks, and laborers. They lined up with Ransom, Murphy, Trenchard, Laler, Case, Thompson, Winslow, Johnson, and Davis. The players all wore cheaply made overalls.

There was only one umpire to officiate at that championship baseball game. He wore a long frock coat.

That game of June 19, 1846, was played not only for the baseball championship of the land, but also for a side wager. The losing team was to buy dinners at an expensive restaurant, with champagne and all the trimmings, for the players of the winning team.

The baseball game started, but it didn't last too long —only four innings. For it had been agreed that the game would be over just as soon as one team made twenty-one runs. The New York Nine players fielded better and hit harder. In four innings, they piled up the necessary twenty-one runs, with two to spare, to win that championship game by a final score of 23–1.

There was only one unpleasant incident during the game. A Knickerbocker player, angered by a close call, berated the umpire, who promptly fined him sixteen cents. The spectators applauded the umpire's display of authority.

Although the Knickerbocker players were all gentlemen to the manner born, the defeat so galled them that five years were to pass before those haughty players consented to engage in another diamond match.

That's all there is to the story of a baseball game played on June 19, 1846.

However, it's a date that became unforgettable in baseball history. Because everything that has happened in baseball since then stems from that baseball game. That was the first match game in baseball history.

In 1902, the great first baseman and player-manager Frank Chance, known as "The Peerless Leader" of the Chicago Cubs, startled the baseball world by installing two rookies in the Cub infield. Both were under twenty years old. Johnny Evers was installed at second base, and Joe Tinker was placed at short. Those two rookies became great pals, as well as the greatest keystone combination in major-league baseball. They made up two thirds of the most fabulous double-play combination of all time, that legendary infield trio of "Tinker-to-Evers-to-Chance"!

One day, shortstop Joe Tinker and second baseman Johnny Evers had a foolish quarrel over a trifling incident. It happened because Evers had taken a hack to the ball park and driven off without offering his pal a ride. So, the two friends stopped talking to each other and, the longer their silence prevailed, the more they grew to dislike each other.

Their feud became the talk of the majors. No one could patch up their broken friendship. Everyone expected that great keystone combination to break up completely. But, although Joe Tinker and Johnny Evers never spoke to each other off the field, they continued to play flawlessly together, side by side, for eleven seasons. In the infield, they played as one, and so efficient were those two as a keystone combination that they paced the Chicago Cubs to four pennants, and two world championships.

But even after their playing days were over, their silent feud continued for twenty-five more years.

Then one day, when both had grown old and weary with the miseries of life—Johnny Evers had become a wheel-chair invalid, and Joe Tinker had lost a leg—they met by chance. For a long moment those two former teammates stared at each other, and then both fell upon each other with hugs and tears, to reclaim their broken friendship.

Now, they dwell side by side, in baseball's Hall of Fame.

BE A CLOWN

In 1947, when the awkward Lawrence "Yogi" Berra came to the major leagues to play for the New York Yankees, everybody laughed at him when he squatted down behind home plate. Even his own manager said then that he looked like an ape and played like a clown. Bench jockeys around the league and even his teammates made sport of him. But Yogi took the cruel "riding" with surprising good nature. When he was taunted for his coarse looks, he simply retorted: "It don't matter if you're ugly in this racket. All you have to do here is hit the ball, and I never saw nobody hit one with his face."

When they laughed at his clumsiness as a catcher, Yogi, who never even had finished grade school, defended himself by saying: "Coach Bill Dickey is learning me how to catch. He's learning me all his experience!"

The baseball world tagged Yogi Berra as an amusing clown, and he never shook off that reputation. But in time, he became one of the best-loved ballplayers in history, a player without an enemy. Surprisingly, down through the years, he became even more than that. He became perhaps the greatest catcher in the history of baseball and one of the most feared batters in major-league annals. He made more hits than any other backstop in history—2148. He hit more home runs than any other catcher in history—358. Yogi Berra also became the highest-paid catcher in major league history and three times winner of the "Most Valuable Player" award.

Even all that wasn't enough glory for the ungainly, uneducated little clown. He also spread himself all over the record book as the most amazing World Series performer of all time. He played in as many World Series classics as anyone and he made more hits than anyone else in World Series history.

Yogi Berra was thirty-eight, and the richest catcher in history when he finally put away his "tools of ignorance" as the catcher's gear is called, and gave up backstopping in the major leagues. In 1964, he had a new job in the big leagues. He had become the manager of the New York Yankees, the greatest pennant-winning club in major-league history, to prove that miracles can happen in baseball. And he piloted them to a pennant, too.

WHEN SUNNY JIM WENT ON A RAMPAGE

"Sunny Jim" Bottomley already had a great runs-batted-in record but he overshadowed it in one afternoon in a single nine-inning game. Swaggering, happy-go-lucky Sunny Jim, who was at first base for sixteen years, was one of the most feared hitters in the game. Season after season he hit well over .300 and his top mark as a batsman was .371!

But on that one day, September 16, 1924, Jim Bottomley's St. Louis Cardinals were playing the Dodgers. In the first inning, when Sunny Jim came to bat, he singled, and drove in two runs. In the second inning, again he came to bat, and he doubled, to drive in another run. In the fourth inning, he came to bat with the bases full, and homered, to drive in four more runs. Now he had seven runs batted in, but he was hardly done for that day. For when he came to bat in the sixth inning, with a teammate on base, he homered again, to drive in two more runs. So now he had a total of nine runs batted in.

When he came to bat in the seventh inning, again there were teammates on base. He singled, and drove in two more runs. In the ninth inning, he came up to bat for his last time in that game. Again he singled, and again he drove in a run. It completed as fantastic a hitting performance as was ever seen in a major-league game. "Sunny Jim" had been up to bat six times in the nine innings, and he had made three singles, a double, and two home runs, off five different pitchers—to bat in an astounding total of twelve runs!

No batter ever swept the bases as thoroughly as did Sunny Jim Bottomley.

THE SPEECHLESS HURLER

Luther "Dummy" Taylor was nobody's dummy on a big-league diamond. He never said a word, nor did he ever hear cheers for himself. He was born a deaf-mute.

Dummy Taylor was twenty-four when he crashed the majors, with the New York Giants. That deaf-mute pitcher wasted no time in showing the big leagues that he was no freak. He became the work horse of the Giants' staff. In 1904, it was Dummy Taylor who, with his twenty-one victories, helped win the first pennant for the Giants, and his rugged pitching helped them win another pennant.

Dummy Taylor remained a big-league pitcher for ten seasons, and he won 116 major-league games. In those years, although he was unable to speak a word or hear one, he was one of the most colorful players in the game. Despite his handicap, that deaf-mute pitcher became one of the most amusing and adroit umpire-baiters in the majors. Silently, he could needle an umpire to distraction.

Dummy Taylor used to "dress down" an umpire in

sign language, and nothing ever happened to him. But once while doing it, he saw the ump gesturing at him. Then, to everyone's surprise, pitcher Taylor left the mound, deflated, and headed for the clubhouse. Later, his puzzled teammates learned what had happened. The abused ump had told Dummy Taylor in his own sign language: "Listen, smart guy, I've gone to school and have learned the sign language, and I can now understand everything you call me. You'll never again call me a blind bum and get away with it. For every time you do, I'll throw you out of the game!"

After his days as a big-league pitcher were over, Dummy Taylor, still in love with baseball, turned to teaching deaf and dumb youngsters how to play the game. He also umpired in pro and college games, and he continued until he was almost eighty. And, while he did, he continued to search for a ballplayer to send to the big leagues. He finally found one in a youngster named Dick Sipek. Dummy Taylor taught him all he knew, and helped him go up to the big leagues, as an outfielder for the Cincinnati Reds. It was a proud day for Dummy Taylor when his find, Dick Sipek, became a major-league player. Dick Sipek was also a deaf-mute.

A HUSBAND FOR THE
CLUB OWNER'S DAUGHTER

In 1925, a gangling, awkward, eighteen-year-old Irish lad from the San Francisco sand lots was given a tryout by the Pittsburgh Pirates. He didn't last long in the majors, and he was quickly shipped to the minors. There a Washington Senators baseball scout spotted him, and, since he had vague orders to pick up anything resembling a shortstop, if the price was low enough, the scout bought that square-jawed Irish youngster for seventy-five hundred dollars.

When the Washington club owner, the late Clark Griffith, was told about that purchase, he was furious with his scout, who had spent so much of the club's money for an obscure minor-league kid who was an awkward shortstop and a weak hitter.

However, the scout tried to "butter up" the angry club owner with a romantic approach. When he brought the rookie shortstop to Clark Griffith's office for a first inspection, he turned to the club owner's daughter, who was present at the time, and happily chirped at her: "Hi ya, Mildred! I been scouting for a husband for you, and have brought you a young sweetie from Kansas City. Meet Joe Cronin!"

Just as it happens in story books, the rookie and the club owner's daughter fell in love and married to live happily ever after. But Joe Cronin had to go a long way before club owner Clark Griffith also fell in love with him—as a ballplayer. The "Old Fox" grumbled quite a bit in the beginning because he wanted the Senators' manager to play another young hopeful at short instead of the awkward Joe Cronin.

As the years went by, the square-jawed Irishman became so great a shortstop that Clark Griffith also made him the manager of the Washington team, even though he was only twenty-eight. And after seven glorious seasons he sold his son-in-law to the Boston Red Sox for two-hundred-fifty thousand dollars—the highest price ever paid for a ballplayer.

Joe Cronin starred as a player-manager in the majors for eleven more years. When his playing days were over, he not only became an important and respected big-league baseball executive, but eventually, he achieved a success never before known by a major-league player. Joe Cronin became the president of the American League.

* * *

Back in the nineteenth century, the baseball world marveled over the exploits of Hugh Daly as a pitcher in the big leagues. In 1883, he hurled a no-hit no-run game, and on another occasion, he struck out nineteen players in a nine-inning contest, which still stands as a major-league record.

That remarkable right-hander, nicknamed "One Arm," won seventy-two games in the National League, even though he was physically handicapped. He was a cripple with no left arm.

* * *

Many mighty and prolific home-run sluggers achieved imperishable baseball fame for their artistic ability to knock the ball out of big-league parks. But John Franklin Baker is now the only immortal in baseball's Hall of Fame who ever acquired the dramatic and colorful nickname of "Home Run" for his skill to belt circuit clouts. Yet, in the thirteen years that ace third baseman starred in the major leagues, Home Run Baker never hit more than twelve homers in any one season.

* * *

Catcher Muddy Ruel, outfielder Johnny Cooney and third baseman Floyd Baker were the three worst home-run hitters in modern baseball history.

As a big-leaguer, Muddy Ruel came to bat 4514 times, but he hit only four home runs. Johnny Cooney had 3364 licks at bat as a major-leaguer, but he hit only two home runs. However, Floyd Baker achieved the fame of being the worst home-run hitter of all time. He came to bat in the majors 2280 times. He hit one home run.

A TRIPLE KILLING

Neal Ball was just a mediocre ballplayer. He was a shortstop and, in the seven seasons he lasted in the Big Show, he was with three different teams. His fielding was spotty, and his season's batting average usually scaled from a puny .172 to a lofty mark of .230.

But on the afternoon of July 19, 1909, Neal Ball, who was shortstopping for the Cleveland Indians in a game against the Boston Red Sox, suddenly became a diamond hero. In the second inning of that game, with the Red Sox at bat, two of their men reached base safely. There was a runner on first and on second, with no outs, and Boston's most dangerous slugger at bat.

He hit a screaming liner heading for the outfield. But luckily, Neal Ball happened to be in the right spot at the right moment. He made a desperate leap high into the air, and caught the ball. The startled runner on second was so far off base on his way to third that Neal Ball simply stepped on the bag and retired him for the second out.

Then, to his surprise, he spotted the runner from first standing bewildered far off the initial sack. So, Neal Ball quickly walked up to him, and tagged him with the ball, to complete the third out for that inning. Thus, singlehanded, shortstop Neal Ball had retired three men in one play, to achieve a startling and unprecedented feat for baseball history. It was baseball's first unassisted triple play!

Even long after his major-league playing days were over, Neal Ball still basked in the glory of his rare feat.

And rare indeed it was! To this day, only six other major-league players have matched Neal Ball's feat of an unassisted triple play.

TWENTY-GAME WINNERS

Blessed is the pennant-hungry team that can turn up two twenty-game winners in the same season. But major-league teams with twenty-game pitching winners haven't always been pennant winners.

In 1923, a pennant-hungry Cincinnati Reds team came up not only with one sensational twenty-game winner, in the famed Cuban, Adolpho Luque, with twenty-seven triumphs, but with two more. For his teammate Pete Donohue won twenty-one games, and his roommate Eppa Rixey won twenty games. But even though that season the Cincinnati team boasted of three twenty-game winners, it didn't wind up with the pennant.

Years ago, the pennant-hungry Cleveland Indians

also came up with three twenty-game winners. The Hall of Famer Bob Feller won twenty-two games, Mike Garcia won twenty, and so did Early Wynn. But the Indians didn't win the pennant that season. The following season, the Cleveland Indians again came up with three more twenty-game winners. For Early Wynn won twenty-three games, Mike Garcia won twenty-two, and so did Bob Lemon. But again, the team wound up the season without a pennant. Four years later, once more the Cleveland Indians came up with three pitchers with twenty wins each—Early Wynn, Bob Lemon, and Herb Score. But again no pennant for the Indians.

Even more astonishing was the frustration of the Chicago White Sox team of 1920. That season, the White Sox featured four twenty-game winners, the most ever assembled on one major-league club in a single season. They were Claude Williams with twenty-two wins; Red Faber, also with twenty-two victories; while Eddie Cicotte and his teammate Dickie Kerr won twenty-one games each. But, even though that White Sox team had four twenty-game winning pitchers, it didn't win the pennant!

THE DAY WOMEN WERE NO LADIES

Once ladies were restricted from big-league baseball games.

But in 1897, the Washington Senators decided to stage a Ladies' Day. The club owner figured that an invitation to ladies to see his team play, for free, would attract perhaps several hundred curious females, and help spread interest in major-league baseball to the weaker sex.

When the gates opened that September afternoon, thousands of women swooped down on the Washington ball park. For all, the object of their presence and interest seemed to be George "Winnie" Mercer, a handsome

pitcher who on that day had been scheduled to hurl for the Washington club.

Early in that game, pitcher Winnie Mercer began to find fault with the umpire's decisions on balls and strikes. The female spectators loudly sided with Winnie Mercer, against the umpire, Bill Carpenter.

In the fifth inning of that game, Winnie Mercer became annoyed with umpire Carpenter, walked up to him and presented him with a pair of eyeglasses. The ladies shrieked with delight. But umpire Carpenter was not amused, and without hesitation, he ordered the handsome pitcher out of the game!

Most of the women in the stands jumped to their feet and screeched their hatred at the umpire. But he ignored their wrath, and the game proceeded without their glamorous hero, Winnie Mercer, on the mound.

But no sooner was the game over than thousands of infuriated females poured out of the stands, shouting threats at the umpire. Whereupon the brave arbiter who never had quailed before the fury of a male mob now became frightened and hastened to cover. Before he could reach the safety of the Washington club house, several women attacked him and tore his clothes. Once inside, umpire Carpenter demanded that the Washington club protect him. So, they bolted the doors and closed the heavy window shutters, as a hail of stones and bricks crashed against the structure. Many of the enraged women used their parasols to beat against the shutters. Some even found clubs with which they tried to break down the door. Another horde of angry females began to vent their rage on the ball park. Seats were ripped out, windows were broken, and railings bent. The police were called, but the women continued. They remained in the ball park until dark, waiting for the umpire. Meanwhile, the frightened arbiter had to be smuggled out of the ball park, to save his life.

Many years were to pass before any other major-league club staged a Ladies' Day in its ball park.

A stingy, tightfisted club owner may have been the cause of an act that destroyed one of the greatest teams in the history of the major leagues and almost nearly ruined big-league baseball.

It began with a broken promise to a once-famous pitcher known in the annals of the game as Eddie "Knuckles" Cicotte.

When he hurled in the majors, it wasn't unusual for him to pitch more than three hundred innings a season, or to win at least twenty games. But, curiously, that pitching great never earned a season's salary of more than thirty-five hundred dollars.

In the 1919 season, when Eddie Cicotte was pitching for the Chicago White Sox, one of the greatest major-league teams in history, he was at his peak as a mound magician. Although receiving a lowly season's salary of only thirty-five hundred dollars, there was a bonus clause in his contract stipulating that should he win thirty games he would be paid an additional five-thousand dollars.

To earn that bonus, Eddie Cicotte pitched his arm off, and, almost three weeks before the end of the season, he not only had led the Chicago White Sox to an easy pennant, but had also won twenty-nine games. All he needed now was just one more victory to collect the promised five-thousand-dollar bonus. There were three more weeks left for him to win that needed thirtieth game.

But events conspired to prevent him from winning that one game he needed to collect his bonus. For day after day, while Eddie Cicotte waited to pitch, his manager failed to call on him for mound duty. When he angrily complained to the club owner and demanded to know what curious shenanigans were going on to cheat him out of the promised bonus, he was curtly told that it was up to the manager to pitch him when he wanted him. And when Cicotte complained to the White Sox pilot, he was told simply: "I'm resting you for the World Series!"

So, Eddie Cicotte, winner of twenty-nine games, sat in the dugout waiting for three weeks for a call to pitch, a call that never came.

No one will ever know the bitterness that was stored up in Eddie Cicotte's heart for being cheated out of a promised five-thousand-dollars bonus. But what is known now is part of baseball history, a shameful part, for in September of 1920, that great Chicago White Sox pitcher confessed to a Cook County grand jury that he had accepted a bribe to "fix" the outcome of the 1919 World Series, which had been lost by the White Sox. Eddie Cicotte never again pitched in organized baseball.

The scandal not only destroyed that great Chicago White Sox pennant-winning team; it also rocked the very foundation of major-league baseball and almost ruined big-league play as a national game!

THE HONEST LITTLE PITCHER

No big-league baseball hero was ever treated more shamefully than Dickie Kerr. Because of it, he was robbed of his chance to become perhaps one of the greatest pitchers in the history of the major leagues.

In 1919, when 130-pound Dickie Kerr came to the big leagues to pitch for the Chicago White Sox, that team was one of the greatest in history. But that tiny left-handed rookie pitcher made the team, and he also became a shining star.

The White Sox club breezed into the pennant. It was a prohibitive favorite to win that World Series. For rookie Dickie Kerr, pitching in that post-season classic was a baseball dream in reality. When he went to the mound to hurl in his first World Series, he pitched his heart out, to win. And he performed an unforgettable hurling feat. He won one game with a three-hit shutout, and a second game with a victory in ten innings. But even little Dickie Kerr didn't realize at the time how miraculous was his feat in winning two games in that 1919 World Series. For he didn't know that, while he was pitching, the White Sox first baseman, shortstop, third baseman, right fielder, and center fielder were all in an evil plot to throw that World Series. For eight of his teammates had sold out to gamblers. The World Series had been fixed for the White Sox to lose. Despite Dickie Kerr's heroic victories, the Chicago White Sox lost.

Later, when the plot was uncovered, the scandal almost ruined major-league baseball. The evil eight players were driven from the game, in shame, and outlawed from baseball for life. However, Dickie Kerr had emerged from that Series a star for the whole baseball world to admire.

He became a symbol for honesty and integrity. As time passed, the midget left-hander enriched his fame as a great big-league pitcher. For in 1920, he won twenty-one games for the White Sox, and in the following season, he won nineteen games for his seventh-place club.

At the end of the 1921 season, the honest pitcher asked his club owner for a living wage. He held out for a season's salary of only thirty-five hundred dollars. But the penurious club owner refused to pay it, and forced Dickie Kerr out of the big leagues. Hurt and bitterly disillusioned, the honest little pitcher quit the majors—forever.

Although big-league baseball had treated Dickie Kerr shabbily and shamefully, nevertheless he didn't lose his love for baseball. For years later, he found a discouraged, unknown young pitcher, and made him into an outfielder. Dickie Kerr's "find" became one of the greatest players of all time. He remained in the major leagues for twenty-two years, and he set sixty-four different baseball records. He was Stan "The Man" Musial.

TOM THUMB
COMES TO THE BIG LEAGUES

One day in 1951, the former St. Louis Browns played a double-header against the Detroit Tigers. Nothing unusual happened in the first game.

But in the second game, when the Browns' first batter appeared, the fans shrieked. The batter was a midget. The forty-three-inch, twenty-six-year-old player named Eddie Gaedel wore a Browns' uniform, bearing Number ⅛—and he was waving the tiniest bat ever seen in a major-league game.

When the plate umpire, Ed Hurley, appeared skeptical and challenged Eddie Gaedel's presence at bat, the

Browns' manager, Zach Taylor, produced a legitimate player's contract signed by Eddie Gaedel. Only then was he permitted to bat.

The startled Detroit pitcher, Bob Cain, was unable to find the strike zone for Eddie Gaedel. Without taking his bat off his shoulder, he drew a base on balls, on four straight pitches.

Upon reaching first base on a walk, Eddie Gaedel was replaced by a pinch runner. By nightfall, the whole baseball world knew of the St. Louis ball park event on that August 19 afternoon. Eddie Gaedel became the most talked-about player in the majors!

On the following day, the president of the league publicly reprimanded the St. Louis Browns' club owner, for hiring so strange a ballplayer. He barred Eddie Gaedel from the majors—forever.

THE CONFIDENT TEACHER

One day when rookie Tommy Holmes, who eventually became a famous slugging outfielder, was at a batting-practice session for the former Boston Braves, manager Casey Stengel stood watching. Stengel watched him hit a few, then stepped forward and said to him: "Look, kid, you don't seem to know how to pull the ball down the first-base line. Now you watch me do it, for when I played, I used to be an expert at pulling the ball to first to get on base."

Manager Stengel grabbed rookie Holmes's bat, and called for a pitch. The hurler on the mound reared back and let fly a high fast ball. It conked Casey Stengel on the head, and he dropped at home plate, almost unconscious. When he finally dragged himself to his feet, he told the worried rookie: "Son, I guess I'd better demonstrate what I was telling you tomorrow. For that lousy wild pitcher of mine just put me on base."

More than ten thousand men have played in the majors since the beginning of big-league baseball. But only nine were major-league players for one day. Strangely, all nine played their only major-league game on the same day and for the same team. It happened because the greatest player in baseball history had lost his temper.

On the afternoon of May 15, 1912, the immortal Ty Cobb, star of the Detroit Tigers, and baseball's greatest player, goaded beyond endurance by a heckling fan, lost his temper, rushed into the grandstand, and beat him nearly unconscious. Ty Cobb was fined one hundred dollars, and he was suspended for ten days.

Aroused over his chastisement, Ty Cobb's teammates demanded that his suspension be lifted, and threatened to strike. Their demands were ignored.

On May 18, the Detroit Tigers were in Philadelphia to play the Athletics, then the world's baseball champions. Hours before the start of that scheduled game, when the Detroit players learned that Ty Cobb's suspension had not been lifted, nineteen Tigers went out on strike. It was the first players' strike in baseball history.

"You've got to play!" manager Hugh Jennings pleaded with his stubborn players. "If we don't show up for today's game, we'll not only lose it by forfeit, but the club will be fined five thousand dollars for failure to field a team."

But the Tigers refused to play, and some of the striking players even set up a picket line outside the ball park, to keep the public away from the game.

The harassed Tiger pilot, suddenly finding himself without a team to field for that afternoon game, set out on a frantic hunt for other players. He found nine Philadelphia sand-lotters who had played together as a semipro team under the name of the Park Sparrows. They were: Aloysius Travers, Jack Coffey, Pat Meany, Hap

Ward, Billy Maharg, Jim McGarr, Dan McGarvey, Bill Leinhauser, and Ed Irwin. Manager Jennings hired them to play that May 18 game for ten dollars each. However, Aloysius Travers, a young collegian studying for the priesthood, was promised twenty-five dollars to pitch for the unknown sand-lotters. The nine "strikebreakers" were garbed in Tiger uniforms, and sent out on the field to play the greatest team in the majors, before an amused crowd of twenty thousand spectators.

It was the most ludicrous major-league game ever played. Although most of the players of the champion Athletics bunted when they came to bat, nevertheless a ground ball knocked out two teeth from the mouth of the Tigers' third baseman, and the Detroit center fielder was knocked unconscious when a fly ball hit him on the head. The game ended with a score of 24–2.

However, that travesty had a sobering effect on the striking Detroit players. They realized that by their mutinous action they were shaking the foundation of major-league baseball. So, even though Ty Cobb remained suspended, the Tigers ended their strike, and went back to work. The nine obscure sand-lotters who had filled in as strikebreakers, were paid off, each was rewarded with an extra twenty dollars, and they all vanished into oblivion.

* * *

An unforgettable day in the history of baseball was April 15, 1910. It was the opening day of a new big-league season, and in the nation's capital, William Howard Taft, the twenty-seventh President of the United States, had come to the ball park to watch the Washington Senators play the Philadelphia Athletics, and to pitch the first ball to start that contest. It was the first time that a Chief Executive of the nation attended and presided at a major-league baseball game.

It inaugurated the custom of American presidents throwing out the first opening-day ball of every new big-league season—now a baseball tradition.

* * *

In 1961, although outfielder Roger Maris hit only a puny .260 for the New York Yankees, he set an all-time home-run record for a single major-league season, by belting sixty-one four-baggers.

TWO STUBBORN PITCHERS

On May 2, 1917, a hurling duel was staged by two over-stuffed pitchers who together packed nearly six hundred pounds.

Fred Toney pitched for the Cincinnati Reds, and Jim "Hippo" Vaughn hurled for the Chicago Cubs.

There were only thirty-five hundred spectators in the stands on that May 2 afternoon to watch the two rival pitching behemoths, huffing and puffing away for a victory.

But, as inning after inning slipped through the scoreboard, everyone realized that he was a lucky witness to the greatest pitching duel in history. For neither right-hander Fred Toney nor southpaw Hippo Vaughn gave up a hit. That was how both came to the ninth inning of that ball game. The crowd froze. Two rival pitchers were actually hurling a no-hitter in the same game.

Hippo Vaughn breezed through the ninth and completed his no-hitter. Now it was up to big Fred Toney to match the feat and complete the miracle of a double no-hitter in one nine-inning game. He did it! So the double no-hitter went into extra innings.

It came to an end in the tenth when the fabulous Indian, Jim Thorpe, the greatest all-around athlete of the twentieth century, who was then the outfielder for Cincinnati, came to bat and broke up the game by driv-

| CHICAGO | 0 | 0 | 0 | 0 | 0 | 0 | 0 | 0 | 0 | 0 |
| CINCINNATI | 0 | 0 | 0 | 0 | 0 | 0 | 0 | 0 | 1 | 1 |

ing in a run. In his half of the tenth, big Fred Toney still held the Cub batters hitless, to complete the longest winning no-hitter in major-league history!

* * *

On the final day of the 1951 major-league season, the New York Yankees, facing the Boston Red Sox, needed one more victory to win the pennant. So, Allie Reynolds tossed 119 pitches and recorded a no-hit no-run game for his fame. It was the only no-hitter ever hurled on the last day of a big-league campaign to win a pennant. Allie Reynolds' hitless performance on that unforgettable September 28, 1951, was most astonishing, because it was the second no-hit no-run game he had pitched that season.

A PRINCE AMONG DIAMOND THIEVES

Maximilian George Carnarius needed only two more years of religious training at a seminary to become a Lutheran minister. But he heard the call of professional baseball and became a shortstop for seventy dollars a month.

It was late September in the 1910 major-league season. The Pittsburgh Pirates were about to engage in their customary morning practice session. An eager young rookie who had joined the Pirates only the night before, following his purchase from a bush-league club, trotted out to shortstop. But he was intercepted by the bow-legged thirty-seven-year-old Honus Wagner, the greatest shortstop of all time, who good-naturedly asked him: "And what would you be doing at shortstop, son?"

"Why, Mr. Wagner," replied the rookie politely, "I'm the Pirates' new shortstop!"

"You're what?" roared the fabulous Honus Wagner. He made a beeline toward the dugout, where player-manager Fred Clarke, a Hall of Fame outfielder, was watching the proceedings.

"Hey, skipper!" roared old man Wagner. "The kid standing out there tells me he's your new shortstop. Well, I'm going to tell you that I'm the shortstop on this club, and I'm going to be the shortstop for many more years! If you want to play this kid, then let him take your place in the outfield. You're thirty-eight and maybe it's time for you to quit anyway!"

So, the rookie shortstop Maximilian George Carnarius was chased into the outfield by the immortal shortstop Honus Wagner, and thus began his long major-league career as one of baseball's greatest outfielders. Better known as Max Carey, he starred in the majors for twenty years, and no major-league player has ever approached him as a base-burglar. For almost a full decade, Max Carey led the National League in stolen bases, and he was rarely caught in his "larceny-act." His total of 738 steals is a modern National League record. In 1922, he stole fifty-one bases in only 53 attempts. It was a performance of precise larceny unmatched by any of the great base-stealers of major-league history.

THE SONG THAT WILL NEVER DIE

Jack Norworth is immortalized in baseball's Hall of Fame even though he never played major-league baseball. His only contribution to the game was a song.

At the turn of the century, Jack Norworth was a well-known song-and-dance man on the vaudeville stage. That period was a glorious era for major-league baseball.

However, Jack Norworth had no interest in baseball and its fabulous heroes. The stage was the love of his life. But strangely enough, he made a more lasting impression on the sport of baseball than many of its greatest stars.

One day in 1908, while riding in New York's subway, on the way to the theater, Jack Norworth chanced to see a poster advertising the major-league games at the famed Polo Grounds. Ever the shrewd showman, he suddenly realized that a song about baseball might have popular appeal. He promptly began to compose lyrics for a baseball song. Before that subway ride had ended, just thirty minutes later, Jack Norworth had written a ballad he called "Take Me Out to the Ball Game!"

The next night, Jack Norworth introduced the new song to his theater public. When he finished, the audience went wild.

The creator of the most popular baseball song ever written, had never seen a big-league game before he composed his famous song, and even after he had written it as a song for the whole world to sing, he had so little liking for the game of baseball, and so little interest in its romance, that almost forty years passed before he went to see his first major-league game played.

That song, which he had written hurriedly during a brief subway ride, became his biggest hit, and it won for him his greatest fame as a song writer of more than three thousand songs. "Take Me Out to the Ball Game" took America by storm. It became the national anthem of the national pastime!

Because of his song, the doors of baseball's Hall of Fame opened to Jack Norworth, so that he could live in spirit with all the diamond immortals dwelling in the sacred shrine at Cooperstown. There is now the original penciled draft of his famous song—a treasured souvenir of baseball history.

THE ONE GAME
HE DIDN'T WANT TO PITCH

Walter Johnson was an eighteen-year-old pitcher on the sand lots of Idaho when a traveling cigar salesman discovered him. Although that eager drummer bombarded major-league club owners with letters extolling the wonders of his pitching discovery, none of the big-league clubs paid any attention to his rave letters. Finally, the Washington Senators picked up Walter Johnson for exactly nine dollars, which was the price of a railroad ticket from Idaho to Washington, D.C.

On August 2, 1907, Walter Johnson made his debut in the major leagues. He lost his first game. But he was to remain in the big leagues for twenty-one years and become perhaps the greatest pitcher of all time. For twelve seasons, ten in a row, he won twenty or more games. Twice he won more than thirty a season. Only he once hurled fifty-six consecutive scoreless innings. Only he pitched 113 shutouts, and completed 531 major-league games.

He was the king of all opening day pitchers. On April 15, 1910, he hurled his first major-league opening game for the Washington Senators. It was a historic occasion because it was the first time a President of the United States attended a big-league baseball game. President William Howard Taft threw out the first ball at that command performance of the national pastime. Walter Johnson won it with a one-hit shutout.

Sixteen years later, on April 13, 1926, the legendary "Big Train" pitched his last opening day game in the majors. Again he won by a shutout in a fifteen-inning mound duel.

Between his first and his last victory, Walter Johnson pitched a record fourteen inaugural day games, and only he ever won nine openers, seven of which were shutouts.

However, in 1920, the great Johnson had the worst season of his big-league career. He won only eight games. But one of them was his most unforgettable victory, and the strangest.

On July first of that year, the "Big Train" came to the ball park suffering with a lame pitching arm, the first and only time in his long career as a major-league pitcher. He could hardly raise it. Nevertheless, because he was the Senators' biggest attraction and, because a huge crowd had come to see him pitch, sore-armed Johnson consented to try hurling an inning or two, so as not to disappoint his admirers.

"If my lame arm gives me too much trouble, I'll quit," he informed his manager.

Although he suffered with every pitch, the Boston Red Sox could not hit his blinding fast ball for the first two innings.

"Try just one more inning," coaxed his manager, at the end of each frame, and the loyal hurler continued to pitch. So it went—inning after inning, until the sore-armed Walter Johnson had twirled a full nine innings. It was the most heroic and most satisfying game ever pitched by a big-league hurler. For, despite his lame arm, Walter Johnson had given up no hits and no runs, to score a no-hitter for his fame.

It was the only no-hit no-run game ever pitched by the immortal Walter Johnson, in the 414 major-league victories he achieved as the "Big Train" of baseball.

TO BET OR NOT TO BET

World Series hero Louis "Bobo" Newsom pitched for fifteen teams in both major leagues in nineteen seasons, and won more than two hundred games. But he was also a celebrated merry clown who was quick to defend his vices.

That wandering character had a weakness for the bangtails. A baseball day rarely passed when Bobo failed to place a bet on a horse race. Eventually, the famous iron-fisted Czar of Baseball, the late Judge Kenesaw Mountain Landis, who abhorred gambling in any form, heard about Bobo's vice, and he promptly called him up on the carpet for a judicial accounting.

"Look here, Newsom," snapped the stern baseball commissioner, "a ballplayer who bets on race horses can't keep his mind on the game! Suppose you're pitching in a tight ball game and have to go to bat in the eighth inning when you've got a big bet going on a horse. What will you be thinking of then, baseball or your bet?"

Pitcher Bobo Newsom looked the tough judge

squarely in the eye, and squelched him with a direct and honest reply:

"Mr. Commissioner, you don't have to worry about that. If it's a tight ball game in the eighth, it's a sure bet ol' Bobo won't be in there batting!"

ALL FOR NOTHING

Since major-league baseball began, thousands of games have been played to a decision. But there was once a major league game played that didn't count and became one of baseball's most unforgettable games. It happened on the afternoon of the first day in May in 1920.

On that day, the former Boston Braves played host to the former Brooklyn Dodgers at Braves Field. The fast-ball pitcher Joe Oeschger went to the mound for the Braves. The Dodgers' curve-ball specialist Leon Cadore opposed him. Neither of the two pitchers was one of the great hurlers of his time. For in his eleven years of hurling in the majors, Cadore won only sixty-eight games, while in his fifteen years of pitching, Oeschger won only eighty-two games. But on that memorable day, Cadore and Oeschger engaged in the most fantastic iron-man pitching duel in baseball history.

As Joe Oeschger walked out to the mound to start the game, the Braves' Hall of Fame shortstop, the late Rabbit Maranville, called out to him: "Make it a fast game, Joe! I want to get home early."

For the first four innings, both pitchers hurled shut-out ball. But in the fifth frame, the Dodgers scored a run. However, the Braves quickly came back and tallied a run in the sixth inning, to deadlock the score. Then Joe Oeschger and Leon Cadore settled down to some tight pitching.

At the end of nine innings, the score was still deadlocked, at one run apiece, and Leon Cadore and Joe

Oeschger were still on the mound, twirling tirelessly.

Into extra innings went that May Day Marathon. Past the fifteenth inning went that game, into the twentieth inning, the twenty-second inning passed, and then the twenty-third and still the history-making clash went on.

Surprisingly enough, the two rival catchers grew so weary that both had to be replaced by substitute backstops. But the two rival pitchers still remained on the mound, twirling brilliantly. By the end of the twenty-sixth inning, Leon Cadore had pitched to ninety-five batters, and he had given up only fifteen hits, while hurling twenty scoreless innings. Joe Oeschger was even better, for he had pitched to only eighty-five batters, allowed only 9 hits, while hurling twenty-one scoreless innings.

At that stage of the proceedings, Umpire Barry McCormick observed that the game had been on for three hours and fifty minutes. Thereupon, at the end of the twenty-sixth inning, with the score tied at 1–1, he called the game on account of darkness.

Thus, came to a finish the longest major league game ever played. It was a diamond contest in which an unbelievable total of 180 men had come to bat, and the two rival pitchers had hurled the fantastic number of fifty-two innings, forty-one of which were scoreless. Yet, that historic game had ended with no winner and no loser. It didn't even count.

* * *

No other baseball player in history performed before as many presidents of the United States as did the immortal Walter Johnson. During his twenty-year career with the Washington Senators, he pitched before William Howard Taft, Woodrow Wilson, Warren G. Harding, and Calvin Coolidge. He won at least one opening-day game for each President.

* * *

In 1952, the thirty-three-year-old Virgil Trucks of the Detroit Tigers was a strange flop as a major-league pitcher. For in that entire baseball season, he won only five games. But incredibly, two of those five victories were no-hit no-run games.

THE BASEBALL TRAINER
WHO SWITCHED TO FAME

When the amazing Chicago White Sox, famed as the "Hitless Wonders," downed the fabulous Chicago Cubs in 1906 and, each White Sox player collected almost two thousand dollars as his share of the World Series jackpot, the success went to the trainer's head.

The trainer, Hiram Connibear, an illiterate, touch-and-rough tobacco-chewing guy. He demanded a small cut of the World Series jackpot.

When he failed to get it. Hiram Connibear quit as trainer of the Chicago White Sox club and found a new job, far away from the major leagues. He became the trainer of the University of Washington football team.

As time passed, the crude, rough ex-trainer of the championship major-league baseball club, began to hear campus rumors that the college was thinking of discharging him and hiring someone who would be both the trainer of the football team and the rowing coach. Although Hiram Connibear had never rowed in his life, nor had he ever seen a rowing shell, nevertheless, he quickly volunteered to coach the Washington University crew.

The days that followed his rash act imposed a terrific hardship upon him. Laboriously, he began to digest books and pictures on the sport of crew rowing. Late every night he would sneak down to the boat house to sit for hours and contemplate on the mysteries of rowing. By the flickering light of a lantern, Hiram Connibear drew crude sketches on paper as he tried to figure out the perfect rowing stroke.

In the meantime, a growing discontent spread throughout the university because it became evident that he knew little about the science of crew rowing. Even his rowing squad rebelled against him.

It was then when the ex-trainer of a pennant-winning major-league baseball club decided to lay his cards on the table and call for a showdown. He summoned his crew squad to a secret meeting in the boat house. Facing his hostile crewmen, in his tough vernacular, he confessed to them how little he knew about rowing and how hard he had tried to learn the mystery of coaching a winning crew. Then, crying unashamedly, tough Hiram Connibear pleaded:

"Men, I beg you to give me a chance. Stick with me for a little while longer, and I promise that you won't regret it. I'll help you become a winning crew."

Before long, Hiram Connibear invented a stroke that revolutionized the sport of crew rowing. It became recognized as the most efficient of all rowing strokes. With the "Connibear stroke" the Washington University crews became the greatest in the sport of rowing, and Hiram Connibear became famous as one of the greatest coaches in the history of college crew rowing.

THE ORIGINAL ANGRY YOUNG MAN

In the summer of 1961, a lonely and unhappy old man of seventy-four, afflicted with cancer, diabetes, and chronic heart disease, checked into Atlanta's Emory University Hospital. He carried with him a million dollars' worth of negotiable securities, which he placed on a table beside his bed, and then covered it with a loaded revolver. Days later, he died, leaving behind him a fortune of more than eleven million dollars, and the legend of a baseball hero who will never be forgotten. He was Tyrus Raymond Cobb.

On a sultry August 30 afternoon, in 1905, the manager of the Detroit Tigers beckoned to a gawky eighteen-year-old rookie who only the day before had been purchased by the club for a paltry five hundred dollars.

"Hey, Cobb," he shouted, "look alive and grab yourself a bat to pinch-hit."

The first time he came to bat against the New York Highlanders, now known as the Yankees, the cocky Ty Cobb, son of a Georgia State Senator, doubled off famed Jack Chesbro, then the greatest pitcher in the majors. Thus began the fantastic saga of the greatest player of the major leagues.

For the next twenty-four years, Ty Cobb was a legend of greatness, savagery, hate, turmoil, and violence never before nor since known in big-league baseball.

He came to the majors an angry boy, driven by a strange and wild fury to become the best ballplayer there ever was. To gain fame and fortune, he became the most hated and most feared player in the game. When he played baseball, he rarely had a friend, but he always had a legion of enemies plotting his downfall. He was so irascible that no teammate would room with him. The fiercest of all diamond competitors and a snarling brawler, he fought countless fist fights with rival players, umpires, heckling fans, and even his teammates. Wherever he played, he aroused such violent hate that often he needed police protection. Once a would-be assassin attacked him with a knife, and another time, a mob of irate fans attempted to kidnap him from a railroad train, to lynch him.

One afternoon when he was winding up his twenty-fourth and final season in the big leagues, during a batting rally, his manager suggested that a pinch-hitter bat in his place, because Ty Cobb was then in a batting slump. But the "Georgia Peach" growled back at him: "Nobody ever hits for Cobb!" He went to bat and lined out a safe hit.

Only Ty Cobb played in 3033 major-league games. He scored 2244 runs. Only he in modern baseball ever stole 892 bases. Only he ever batted over .300 for twenty-three seasons. Three times he hit over .400 and only he ever won a major-league batting championship twelve times—nine years in a row. Only he compiled a lifetime batting average of .367—the highest of all time. And only he ever set as many as ninety different baseball records for his fame.

During his final season, Ty Cobb finished with a .323 batting average, and an unbelievable lifetime total of 4191 hits—an all-time record for hits that no player has approached, or ever will.

Although he was so villainous, so conceited, so arrogant, and so disliked, he was the first player to be elected to baseball's Hall of Fame, as the greatest of all the immortals of the game.

Now in the town of Royston, Georgia, the birthplace of the "Georgia Peach," the Ty Cobb Memorial Shrine has been built in memory of the greatest baseball hero there ever was.

THE FIRST BONUS BABY

Baseball's first "bonus baby" was the greatest all-around athlete of all time! He was the immortal Indian Jim Thorpe! And he became the original "bonus baby" only because he played in a forbidden baseball game.

In his time, Jim Thorpe was perhaps the greatest football player and track-and-field performer of all time. And in the 1912 Olympic Games, he became the only athlete in history to win both the Decathlon and the Pentathlon, a contest of fifteen gruelling track-and-field events in competition against the world's greatest athletes.

When Jim Thorpe returned home from the 1912 Olympics, hailed as the world's greatest all-around athlete, someone discovered that once he had played in an obscure baseball game for which he had received twenty-five dollars for expenses. For that crime, the fabulous Jim Thorpe was humiliated by being outlawed from the amateur athletic world. So, the legendary big-league manager, John J. McGraw of the old New York Giants, persuaded Jim Thorpe to sign up as a major-league outfielder, and gave him a fat bonus of nine thousand dollars to turn big-league ballplayer. Thus did the immortal Jim Thorpe become the first "bonus baby" in major-league history because this marked the first time a rookie player was paid a cash bonus to sign a major-league contract.

Jim Thorpe created such a sensation in the major leagues that crowds flocked to ball parks to see him play; although Jim Thorpe was a good outfielder, there was widespread disappointment at his performance because everybody expected him to perform diamond miracles!

He lasted seven years in the majors, and in his final season he attained his highest batting mark when he hit .327! But baseball's first "bonus baby" finally became unwanted by the big leagues, and he devoted himself to playing pro football, a game in which he remained a sensation for twenty years.

THE HUNCHBACK
OF THE MAJOR LEAGUES

The bat boy has always been the most unobtrusive figure in baseball, although a few have achieved a measure of success as ballplayers in the big leagues. Eddie Bennett was just such an exception. By a cruel quirk of nature, he became the most famous bat boy of all time.

Eddie Bennett was a hunchback. As is usually the way with youngsters, the boys of his neighborhood teased him and made him the butt of their jokes.

To escape the cruel jibes and ease his misery and loneliness, the little hunchback began hanging around his home-town big-league ball park, where he could watch the famous major-league players come in and out of the clubhouse.

One afternoon, the famous Chicago White Sox outfielder Happy Felsch happened to see the sad-faced hunchback as he was about to enter the ball park, and, to satisfy a superstitious whim, he gave his hump a playful rub. That day the White Sox won the game, with Happy Felsch starring in it.

The next afternoon, Happy Felsch deliberately looked for the little hunchback as he was about to enter the ball park. When he found him, he happily took him inside, and brought him to the White Sox dugout to meet the other players. Playfully, they all rubbed the hunchback's back for luck, and Chicago won that game. So, Eddie Bennett, by popular acclaim, was made the bat boy and official mascot of the Pale Hose.

With the now-happy hunchback as their bat boy, the Chicago White Sox won the pennant and the 1917 World Series.

The lucky charm of hunchback Eddie Bennett as a bat boy spread far and wide. Other major-league clubs made tempting offers for his services, and finally, the old Brooklyn Dodgers weaned him away with a fancy salary. When Eddie Bennett left the Chicago White Sox, that great team was rocked by a shocking gambling scandal and fell apart. On the other hand, he brought luck to the Brooklyn team, for with him as their bat boy, the Dodgers won the pennant.

Then, the New York Yankees took hunchback Eddie Bennett away from the Dodgers by paying him an even larger salary. It was a higher salary than many well-known major-league players earned in a season. Again the charm of the little hunchback worked wonders —with Eddie Bennett as their bat boy, the Yankees won three straight pennants. Then, after a two-year pause, they again won three pennants in a row, and three consecutive World Series championships, without the loss of even a single game.

No one ever became more famous, nor was paid as much money as Eddie Bennett received during his glory years as a big-league bat boy—the sad-faced hunchback who, because of his handicap, became the most unforgettable bat boy in baseball history.

THE RIGHTEOUS SKIPPER

The Honorable Judge Emil Fuchs owned the old Boston Braves during America's great depression. When the manager's post fell vacant, the thrifty club owner decided to economize by taking over as the pilot of his own team. Although that eminent and pompous jurist knew little or nothing of diamond strategy, nevertheless, the sporting judge believed that a manager's job was a luxury that easily could be dispensed with.

With Judge Emil Fuchs as their dugout skipper, the Braves lost games with monotonous regularity. Finally there came a day when the winless Braves were within reach of a victory, and manager Fuchs had to make a decision to help clinch it.

That afternoon, the hapless Braves came into the last half of the ninth inning with the score tied, and a man on third with the winning run. It was veteran Joe Dugan's turn at bat.

As that famous infielder picked up a club for his lick at bat, he said to manager Fuchs: "Judge, that green kid third baseman of theirs is playing too far back. I'm going to drop a bunt toward third and we'll squeeze in the winning run."

But the good and honest judge was outraged.

"Mr. Dugan, you'll do no such thing!" he snapped angrily. "I want to win this game as much as any of you. But as long as I'm the manager of this team, we'll win fairly and honorably, or not at all!"

A PENNANT LOST BY A FORFEIT

On September 7, 1889, when the old Brooklyn Dodgers and the St. Louis team were locked in a tie for the flag, a large crowd of frenzied fans packed the stands to watch that deciding contest for the pennant!

The St. Louis team jumped into an early lead and for seven innings sat on top of a score of four runs to two. Victory seemed certain for St. Louis as the eighth inning began. But suddenly, the sky clouded, and a creeping darkness enveloped the playing field. The St. Louis players began to clamor for the umpire to call the game on account of darkness. The Dodgers were equally vociferous in demanding that the game be continued even though it had become too dark to play.

For his part, the umpire seemed to be in no hurry to stop the contest, having only two more innings to play. He ordered that the game be continued. Whereupon the St. Louis third baseman, Arlie Latham, a famous diamond clown in his time, decided to force the issue with the stubborn umpire. He ordered the bat boy to bring him a dozen large candles. When he had them, the clowning St. Louis star lined up the twelve candles in front of the St. Louis dugout and lit them.

106

The crowd roared with laughter at that pointed hint to the stubborn umpire. Annoyed and embarrassed, the umpire came over to the St. Louis dugout, and blew out the twelve candles. But no sooner did he return to his position when Arlie Latham again lit them. Once more the umpire came over and blew out all the candles. And again clowning Arlie Latham sneaked out of the St. Louis dugout and lit them. That amusing act continued for several minutes, until the puffing umpire sternly warned the St. Louis players to "cut out" the comedy, and get on with the game. However, Arlie Latham sneaked out of the dugout and lit the twelve candles a fourth time.

It was then that the stubborn umpire really blew his top. In a roaring voice heard all over the ball park, he announced that he had forfeited the game against St. Louis, and the Dodgers were the winners of that contest by a forfeit score of 9–0.

A free-for-all riot followed that weird decision. But the forfeit stood, and the Brooklyn Dodgers, even though they had been trailing by a score of 4–2 when the game was stopped, captured the deciding game for the pennant—by the grace of a forfeit!

WHEN THE YANKEE
CLIPPER SAILED TO GLORY

On the afternoon of May 15, in the 1941 pennant campaign, outfielder Joe DiMaggio of the New York Yankees went to bat four times in a game against the Chicago White Sox, and he squeezed out just one safe hit off a mediocre pitcher named Edgar Smith. But it wasn't an achievement for special sports-page notice, because Joe DiMaggio was the American League batting champion.

However, at that time, little did the baseball world realize the importance of DiMaggio's single safe hit on that afternoon. It was the beginning of a hitting streak never equaled. As Joe DiMaggio continued to hit safely in every game for the balance of that month, few paid attention to his hitting spree.

He continued to hit safely in every game he played all through the month of June, and as his hitting streak grew longer and longer, the baseball world suddenly awoke to the realization that unprecedented batting history was being made. Joe DiMaggio caught up with the hitting streak of thirty-three games in a row, set by the immortal Rogers Hornsby, the greatest right-handed hitter of all time. Then, he caught up with George Sisler's record of forty-one games in a row, and finally, he caught up with the Wee Willie Keeler's hitting record of forty-four games in a row, which had stood unmatched for forty-four years.

He carried his fantastic hitting streak past all the flagpoles erected by baseball's greatest hitters. Finally, in a game on July 17, the fabulous "Yankee Clipper" went to bat four times, and he failed to hit safely even once. It ended the longest hitting streak ever achieved by a major-league player. It had lasted two months and two days. Joe DiMaggio had hit safely in fifty-six consecutive major-league games.

During his unbelievable hitting streak, he had gone to bat 223 times, had belted fifteen home runs, four three-baggers, sixteen doubles, and fifty-six singles, for a total of ninety-one hits. He also had batted in fifty-five runs, and personally scored fifty-six times.

The hitting streak helped the New York Yankees to win the pennant by the staggering margin of seventeen games.

Few players in the history of the major leagues ever had as many big days at bat as did the immortal Stan Musial. He won the National League batting championship seven times in twenty-two years in the big leagues, and he is the only player in history to ever hit five home runs in a single day. He wound up with a career total of 3,630 hits.

In 1948, "Stan the Man" had four unforgettable days of batting glory. On each of those days, he made five hits in five times at bat. The fourth time he achieved that feat, he performed the most astonishing and precise exhibition of perfect batting ever seen on a big-league diamond.

It was the afternoon of September 22, and Musial's St. Louis Cardinals were playing the former Boston Braves. It was a chilly windy day, and Stan Musial was in poor shape. Three days earlier he had hurt his left wrist trying to make an impossible catch in the field. His manager advised him to rest, but Musial wanted to play that day because he was on the way to winning another batting title. (He did win it at that season's end with a .376 batting average.)

Because he knew he shouldn't pull the ball in order to protect the wrist, he had decided not to waste any swings when he came to bat. His first time up in that game and on his first swing at the ball, he hit a single. The next time up, he took just one swing at the pitch and hit a double. Now suffering extreme pain, he came to bat for his third time, and again he took only one swing at the ball and belted a home run—his thirty-eighth of that season. When he came to bat for his fourth time, he poked a single for his fourth hit in a row. Finally, he came up for his fifth time—and again he hit safely!

It completed a perfect day at bat for him—five for five. That was the most incredible feat of perfect hitting ever achieved by a major-league player. In that unforgettable game, Stan Musial came to bat five times and took only five swings at the ball. He made no fouls nor did he miss any strikes.

FROM THE TOP
OF THE WASHINGTON MONUMENT

Only one ballplayer ever achieved fame for catching a baseball coming from a great height, generally an old baseball stunt.

The record catch was caught by William "Pop" Schriver. Before the turn of the century he was one of the best catchers in the big leagues. In 1894, when Pop Schriver was a backstop for the Chicago Cubs, on a visit to the nation's capital to see the famed Washington Monument, Pop Schriver made a boast that he could catch a baseball thrown from its top—555 feet high.

That boast was overheard by the once-famous big-league pitcher, Clark Griffith, who eventually not only founded the American League, but also became the owner of the Washington Senators club. Clark Griffith offered to wager twenty-five dollars that Pop Schriver couldn't perform the stunt.

On the morning of August 25, 1894, pitcher Clark Griffith went to the top of the Washington Monument and tossed down a baseball for Pop Schriver to catch. On his very first try, Pop Schriver caught the ball from that height of 555 feet—and won his bet.

However, that Cub catcher gained no fame for achieving that unusual stunt because hardly anyone had seen him perform it, and later, when he told his teammates and other ballplayers about it, they wouldn't believe him.

Fourteen years later, when catcher Charles "Gabby" Street, playing for the Washington Senators, heard about Pop Schriver's stunt, he boasted that he, too, could

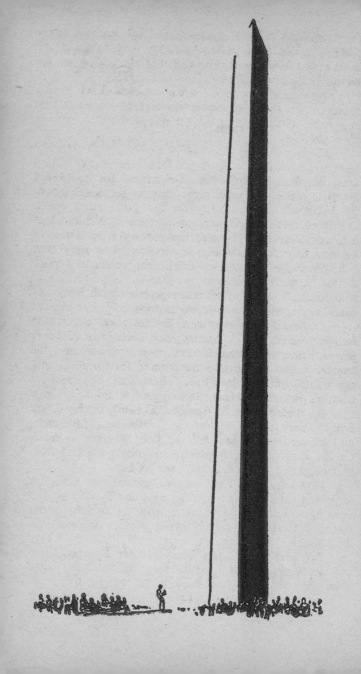

do it, and he offered to wager his full season's salary that he could catch a baseball thrown from the top of the Washington Monument. There was lively betting on the success or failure of that baseball stunt.

On August 21, 1908, when catcher Gabby Street showed up at the Washington Monument to attempt "the impossible catch," a huge crowd was on hand to witness his performance.

Although Gabby Street missed catching the first few baseballs thrown from the top of the Washington Monument, he finally caught one. The crowd wildly cheered his feat, and by the following morning the whole country knew all about Gabby Street's great stunt catch. Overnight, he achieved widespread fame as a miraculous catcher. Wherever he went, and whatever he did as a big-league catcher, he was mostly known as the "Man Who Had Caught a Baseball Thrown from the Top of the Washington Monument!"

However, in 1940, catcher Hank Helf of the Cleveland Indians caught a baseball thrown from a height of seven hundred feet. And the highest stunt catch ever achieved was made by another Cleveland Indians player, named Joe Sprinz. He caught a ball dropped from a height of eight hundred feet. The force of that sky-high catch broke his jaw.

But of all who ever achieved fame for catching a baseball thrown from a great height, only Gabby Street is remembered.

It all began on a day in July in 1914, when a left-handed nineteen-year-old youngster from an orphanage made his debut as a major-league pitcher for the Boston Red Sox. The southpaw lasted seven innings, and he received credit for his first big-league victory, a 4–3 decision over the Cleveland Indians.

He won just one more game in that season before he was shipped off to the minors for more seasoning. The young southpaw was back with the Red Sox the following season, and he began to blossom as a great major-league pitcher. He won eighteen games, and twenty-three the next season, and twenty-three more games the season after that. Eight times that Red Sox southpaw hooked up in mound duels with the immortal Walter Johnson, the second winningest hurler of all time, and he won six of those eight mound contests. Three of those games were won by 1–0 scores.

The left-hander did even more to establish himself as one of the great pitchers of his time. In 1916, he not only hurled the Red Sox to a pennant, but in the World Series he pitched and won a fourteen-inning battle. It still stands as the longest-pitched winning game in classic history.

Two years later, again he helped his team win the pennant, and in that World Series, he won two games, and emerged from that classic with a record of hurling 29⅔ runless innings.

The baseball world acclaimed him as one of the great pitchers of his time. Everyone believed that he was destined to go on to glory as an immortal hurler. The only one who disagreed was his teammate, Harry Hooper, who at the time was one of the greatest outfielders in the game. Curiously, he believed that the young sensational southpaw hurler had a greater future in baseball—as a mighty slugger.

Harry Hooper began to pester the Red Sox manager, Ed Barrow, to shift his spectacular winning left-hander to the outfield, so that he would be able to play every day, and hit. But the Red Sox pilot dismissed the foolish idea, protesting that he would be crazy to convert the best southpaw pitcher in the game into an outfielder of dubious worth.

"If I guessed wrong and this shift didn't work out, I'd be laughed out of baseball," manager Barrow told outfielder Harry Hooper. But the famous Red Sox outfielder continued to argue so convincingly that eventually, manager Barrow relented and consented to make the shift.

It was a phenomenal switch in major-league history. The great Red Sox pitcher remained in the outfield for the next seventeen years, and he not only became one of the greatest right-fielders in history, but the most fantastic home-run slugger of all time. No one before or since has ever smashed out such awesome home runs. His slugging revolutionized the game, and changed big-league baseball, physically, tactically, and financially. For thirteen consecutive seasons, he belted more than forty homers a year, three times more than fifty a season, and in 1927, he amazed the baseball world by becoming the first player in history to slug sixty home runs in a single season. Only he ever hit two or more homers in a single game—72 times.

His fantastic flow of circuit clouts not only earned for him a fortune of millions, but also made him the most famous, the most colorful, and the most lovable baseball hero of all time. He wound up the greatest home-run hitter in the history of baseball. Only he hit an unforgettable total of 729 four-baggers for his everlasting fame. He was the immortal Babe—George Herman Ruth.

FIRST GAMES DON'T ALWAYS COUNT

The most successful rookie pitcher in the history of the major leagues was a twenty-four-year-old freckle-faced, redheaded farm boy from Nebraska. In 1911, the Philadelphia Phillies bought him for five hundred dollars. On April 15 of that season, he made his debut in the big leagues. He lost his first game. Nevertheless, he became the most spectacular and most winning freshman pitcher of all time. In that pennant campaign of 1911, he set a record for victories which stands to this day. He won twenty-eight games.

And to prove that he was no flash in the pan, that amazing rookie pitcher remained in the major leagues for twenty seasons, won 373 games, and wound up an immortal in baseball's Hall of Fame. His name was Grover Cleveland Alexander.

THE STRANGEST
FOOT RACE FOR A BALLPLAYER

Third baseman Hans Lobert was the first major-league player to circle the bases in thirteen seconds.

And in 1913 in a California ball park, more than ten thousand fans assembled to watch Hans Lobert run around the bases in a special race. His opponent was a horse! The late umpire Bill Klem was the starter and judge of that race. Ballplayer and horse stood at home plate waiting for the signal. Umpire Klem fired a gun, and off they went around the bases. To home plate they came, nose to nose. But that famous umpire, who set a legend for "never calling one wrong," declared the horse to be the winner of that race—by a nose! It touched off a mob riot in that ball park. For heavy had been the betting on Hans Lobert to win, and all but the ump thought that he had won the race.

Years later, however, Hans Lobert ran an even more unusual foot race to prove to the baseball world that he was the fastest player in the majors. That race took place in early March, at Havana, Cuba.

The contenders were Hans Lobert, two horses, two automobiles, two motorcycles, and a professional runner. It was a handicap race. The automobiles and motorcycles had to cover seven eighths of a mile, the two horses had to cover six furlongs, and the professional runner and Hans Lobert had to run 535 yards. The winner of that bizarre race was to receive a purse of five hundred dollars.

There were many big-league ballplayers in Havana at the time, and so, there was a lot of wild betting. All of the baseball money was wagered on Hans Lobert to win. Even Hans Lobert's wife, unknown to him, wagered a sizable hunk of the family fortune on her speedy husband, who was famed as the fastest man in the majors.

The race started. Hans Lobert broke fast and took the lead against all his opposition. And he stayed in the lead until he had crossed the finish line. For winning that curious race, he earned more than his entire year's salary as a major-league star. He collected not only the five-hundred-dollar cash prize, but part of the winnings of all the baseball men who had bet on him. No other big-league ballplayer ever collected as much money for running one foot race as did Hans Lobert.

NO PRAYERS FOR THE DEACON

Pitching has always been the most important factor in every World Series. The team with the best pitchers always has emerged from the classic, baseball champions of the world.

To pitch and win one or two games in a World Series, is a glowing achievement. But to pitch and win three games in a single World Series is truly an heroic feat. In all World Series history, less than ten pitchers are listed as three-game winners.

There was once a pitcher who even went beyond winning three complete games in one World Series. He was Charles Phillippe, once known as the Deacon.

It happened in 1903, in the first modern World Series played. The two teams were the Boston Red Sox and the Pittsburgh Pirates. That post-season classic was the best of nine games.

Since Deacon Phillippe had won twenty-five games for the Pirates that season, he was given the honor of hurling the opening game. He faced the immortal Cy Young, the most adept major-league pitcher of all time. But the Deacon outpitched him and won his first game of that World Series.

Two days later, the Deacon was back on the mound. Again he pitched a complete game, and won. When those two teams met to play the fourth game of that World

Series, once again Deacon Phillippe went to the mound, again he pitched a full game, and again he won. In the first four games of that classic, the amazing Deacon pitched three complete games, and he won all three—to become the first pitcher in World Series history to win three games.

It was such an heroic feat that the frenzied crowd spilled out of the stands, hoisted the Deacon up on the shoulders of admiring rooters, and paraded him around the ball park. Then, for more than an hour after that game was over, the Deacon had to stand in the center of the ball field and personally greet all his admirers who had lined up to shake hands with him.

In spite of this victory, the Pirates needed two more. Since none of the other Pittsburgh hurlers could produce them in the fifth and sixth games of that World Series, the weary Deacon went to the mound to pitch the seventh game. He pitched the full nine innings, but he lost. The Pittsburgh manager was desperate. So, back to the mound went the tireless Deacon. He hurled gallantly and well, for he allowed only eight hits, but he lost the game by shutout, and the Pirates lost that World Series.

It was a bitter and frustrating finish for the amazing Deacon, who, of the eight games played in that classic, pitched five complete games for his team, and won three.

THE MITE WHO TURNED INTO A GIANT

"Diamond mites" are no novelty, but "Wee Willie" Keeler was a unique one. He was unquestionably the tiniest ball player in major-league history, standing only sixty-three inches from the ground, and he barely tipped 135 pounds.

It was in 1892 when Willie Keeler was first seen in a major-league game. The club owner thought someone was playing a joke on him. When he saw tiny Willie

Keeler go out to the outfield, he jumped to his feet and shouted: "Get that bat boy out of there!"

"That's not a bat boy," replied the manager of the team, "He's our center fielder!"

But it wasn't long before the whole baseball world came to respect and admire the diamond pygmy. Besides becoming a great outfielder, Keeler turned himself into an expert batter. In fact, there was nothing he could *not* do when it came to place hitting, and the diminutive Irishman became immortalized as the man "who hit 'em where they ain't!"

It took remarkable baseball greats to break the amazing hitting records little Willie Keeler set in his time. His feat of hitting safely in forty-four consecutive games stood for forty-four seasons until Hall of Famer Joe DiMaggio topped it with a mark of fifty-six. His 243 hits in one season stood for fourteen years until immortal Ty Cobb topped it. And his 199 singles made in one season is a record that still stands.

The tiniest player in major-league history compiled batting averages almost beyond belief—.340—.347—.364—.367—.376—.379—.392—.394—and his top batting mark for a season was a phenomenal .432! For his sixteen years in the majors, Willie Keeler compiled a .345 lifetime batting average!

Wherever the little man went, pennants followed him. He was on five championship teams. So famous was he in his time that he was paid a five-figure salary—tops in those old baseball days.

No "diamond mite" ever went as far on the glory road as the outfielder Wee Willie Keeler—the tiniest immortal in the hallowed diamond shrine.

* * *

Beyond all doubt, the legendary Babe Ruth was the most famous, the most important, and the most universally admired baseball player who ever lived. His spectacular diamond heroics not only saved the major leagues from ruin in their darkest hour, but also revolutionized the game for its greatest glory and profit. Even though he set thirty-four regular season records and twenty-six World Series records during his twenty years in the majors, ironically, he never once received the coveted annual honor of the "Most Valuable Player" award.

* * *

In their time, Babe Ruth and his teammate Lou Gehrig were famed in history as the King and the Prince of home-run sluggers. For together they belted 1233 homers for their immortal glory. But on April 2, 1931, in an exhibition game in Chattanooga, Tennessee, they were humbled by the pitching of Jackie Mitchell, who struck out both on only six pitched balls. What was so humiliating about that? Jackie Mitchell was a girl.

A SIT-DOWN STRIKE IN A WORLD SERIES

In 1918, big-league baseball was in bad shape. The world was at war, and many major-league players were in military service. Nevertheless, the pennant campaign went on in both major leagues, until the ruling powers of the game ordered that the season he brought to an end on September 1. So, on Labor Day of 1918, that pennant campaign finished, with the Chicago Cubs winning the flag in the National League, and the Boston Red Sox capturing the pennant in the American League.

The two pennant winners of that short season clashed in a World Series that started on September 5, and ended by September 11. It was a classic with the strangest climax in history.

At the end of the first four games played, the two teams were deadlocked for the world championship. Each club had won twice. The players were disgruntled, and unhappy. For the first four games had been washouts at

the gate, and the players realized that they would wind up with little money for their share of the World Series pot.

A couple of hours before it was time to play the fifth game of that World Series, the players staged a sit-down strike. They simply refused to play until they were promised a larger cut of the World Series receipts.

For more than an hour a strike committee, representing the players of both pennant winners, argued with the club owners and the presidents of both leagues, while thousands of fans in the ball park impatiently yelled for the game to begin. Finally, the striking players were persuaded to be loyal to their club, the public, and the game itself, by giving up their stubborn demands for a larger cut of the gate receipts. The rebellious players suited up, and went out to play. That World Series finished on September 11, with the Boston Red Sox winning the championship, four games to two.

The winning Red Sox players received $1108.45 each, while the losing Chicago Cub players received $671.00 each. It was the poorest payoff for winner and loser in World Series history.

TREAT MOTHER KINDLY ON MOTHER'S DAY

On a day in August of the 1936 season, an eighteen-year-old farm boy made his major-league debut. It was the greatest pitching "first" ever recorded. The phenomenal farm boy struck out fifteen men.

Three seasons later, when he had become an established pitching star of the majors, he decided to bring his mother to the ball park so that she would see him pitch in a major-league game. He brought her to the ball park on Mother's Day of 1939. It was a happy son who had seated her in a private box, close to the playing field, so that she could watch him closely. The thrill of it promised her a rare Mother's Day gift.

That day, the ball park was jammed to the rafters, but the proudest and happiest fan of all was the mother of the famous farm-boy pitcher. The game started. As usual, the farm-boy hurler pitched magnificently. However, in an early inning a rival batter swung desperately at one of his fast balls, and managed to clout a foul that went sailing into the crowded stands. Fans ducked to escape the flying ball, but as an ironic fate would have it, out of all the thousands of spectators in that ball park, that foul ball found the mother of the famous farm-boy pitcher, struck her on the head, and knocked her unconscious.

She was rushed to a hospital. It was a shaken and frightened son who kept vigil at his mother's bedside, until he was assured by the doctors that she was out of danger. He blamed himself for her injury, and he even thought of giving up pitching. But when his mother regained consciousness she comforted her famous son by saying: "Don't blame yourself for what happened today. That freak accident was no fault of yours. Forget it, and go on pitching, and be the great baseball player they all say you are!"

So, the farm boy forgot the horror of that freak accident which had almost cost his mother's life and went on to become one of the greatest pitchers in history!

He pitched three no-hit no-run games, twelve one-hit games, struck out 2,538 batters, and in his seventeen seasons in the majors he won 262 games.

To climax the glory of his pitching achievements, he was enshrined in baseball's Hall of Fame, as an immortal of the game. For his name was Bobby Feller.

THE BALD-HEADED FARMER

Shortly before the start of the 1927 major-league season, the late Ed Barrow, then the builder of the New York Yankees' pennant dynasty, while reading a baseball newspaper, came across an item that read: "William Wilcy Moore, a pitcher for the Greenville club, won 30 games and lost 4."

Intrigued, he made inquiries and was informed that the unknown pitcher Wilcy Moore was an eccentric dirt farmer from the town of Hollis, Oklahoma, who at times did a bit of pitching in the "bushes" to earn an extra dollar. The boss of the famed Yankees figured that any hurler who could win thirty games in any league, however obscure, must have something on the ball. So, sight unseen, he bought that pitcher for twenty-five hundred dollars.

When farmer Wilcy Moore came to the Yankees for the start of the 1927 season, boss Ed Barrow had misgivings about his bargain purchase. For the pitcher was a bald-headed, strange-looking character. Although, he claimed to be only thirty, he looked at least a very tired forty. Moreover, he couldn't throw a curve.

However, Wilcy Moore quickly made a big hit with the Yankee players. Babe Ruth took a shine to him and they became roommates. The mighty "Bambino" loved to tease pitcher Moore about his hitting, for he was probably the worst hitter in baseball history. Babe Ruth bet him five-hundred dollars to fifteen-dollars that Wilcy Moore wouldn't ever make five hits in one baseball season.

In his first season in the majors, the bald-headed dirt farmer from Oklahoma performed an unexpected miracle. He became the greatest relief hurler in the majors! He appeared in fifty games for the Yankees, won nineteen for himself, and he saved that many more for the team. Because of relief pitcher Wilcy Moore, the Yankees breezed into the pennant, and captured the World Series in four straight games. Wilcy Moore was responsible for two of the victories. For his fantastic rookie season, the Yankees paid him a salary of only eighteen-hundred dollars.

He completed his first season in the majors not only in a blaze of glory as the most successful relief pitcher in history, but also as a hitter. For on the last day of that season, Wilcy Moore garnered his fifth safe hit, and he won the five-hundred-dollar bet from Babe Ruth, who had teaased him as the worst hitter of all time. When pitcher Wilcy Moore returned to his farm, he wrote a letter to his roommate Babe Ruth, and told him that, with the five-hundred dollars he had won from him, he had bought a fine pair of jackasses, and that he had named one "Babe" and had named the other "Ruth."

The fabulous, good-natured Babe Ruth got a big kick out of his roomie's revenge.

Wilcy Moore remained to pitch in the majors for seven seasons, and when he finally disappeared from the big leagues, he left behind him an unforgettable reputation.

THE TERRIBLE-TEMPERED LEFTY

Hall of Famer Moses "Lefty" Grove, a winner of three-hundred major-league games, was not only one of baseball's greatest pitchers, but notorious for his temper.

In 1931, Lefty Grove was the ace hurler for the world champion Philadelphia Athletics. During that pennant campaign, with the Athletics roaring on to another flag, terrible-tempered Lefty Grove had much to be calm and happy about. He had run up a winning streak of sixteen straight! It was an American League record. However, Lefty Grove wanted more glory. He himself wanted to hold the major-league record for consecutive victories. So, one afternoon, he went to the mound to pitch against the former St. Louis Browns, then one of the weakest teams in baseball. He expected to easily win his seventeenth straight game.

That afternoon "Old Mose" was never better as a speed-ball pitcher. From the first to the ninth inning, he was magnificent. But in the final frame, Jim Moore, a substitute outfielder for the Athletics, misjudged an easy fly ball, with a runner on base, and, because of it, Lefty Grove lost that ball game, by a score of 1–0.

Grove stomped off the field and returned to the dressing room. He shouted at his teammates, threw gloves and shoes at the walls, broke benches with his violent kicks, and then, he ripped locker after locker from the walls. Lefty Grove's temper tantrum was so fierce that the luckless outfielder Jim Moore, who had made the fatal error that had lost the game, hid in the showers. He was afraid of being attacked by the angry pitcher.

Lefty Grove left the clubhouse in shambles! He went home in a rage and stayed away from the ball park for several days, refusing to talk to his manager or any of his teammates. Finally, the terrible-tempered Lefty Grove stopped sulking at home and returned to pitch for the Athletics. He pitched so well that he wound up that season, with thirty-one wins and only four defeats. It was the best winning percentage ever achieved by a big-league pitcher in a single season, in the twentieth century!

WHAT DID HE EXPECT?

One day during his eleven seasons in the major leagues Stanley "Frenchy" Bordagaray had a tiff with an umpire. Frenchy, known for his antics, ended the argument by spitting in the ump's eye. But it wasn't funny, as the celebrated clown quickly discovered. He was fined five hundred dollars and suspended for sixty days. The chastened Frenchy Bordagaray issued just one public statement in his defense.

"Okay, maybe I did wrong spitting in an ump's eye. But the penalty is a little more than I expectorated."

THE RUBE WAS NO HAYSEED

For more than half a century, baseball's greatest pitchers have tried to match the winning streak that Rube Marquard achieved in a single season. But all have failed.

Yet surprisingly, Richard "Rube" Marquard came to the majors only as an eleven-thousand-dollar purchase. But for years, the baseball world mocked and ridiculed him as the "Eleven-Thousand-Dollar Lemon."

In 1908, the angular left-hander came to the New York Giants from a minor-league club. The nickname "Rube" in no way described Marquard; he wasn't fresh off a farm. He was tall, dark, and handsome, a classy dresser, and a big-leaguer just made for the bright lights of Broadway. It didn't take the Rube very long to impress the sports world with his dash and glamour. A bon vivant, he became celebrated as one of the ten best-dressed men in America, and married a famous stage beauty. Rube even took a fling at the stage himself, singing the popular songs of the time.

However, Rube Marquard made a less favorable impression on the pitcher's mound. During his first three seasons in the majors, he won only nine games. He was promptly tagged with the humiliating label of the "Eleven-Thousand-Dollar Lemon!" But the Giants refused to give up on him. And it was well that they didn't. In 1911, the Rube came into his own. He won twenty-four games and nailed down a pennant for his team. The next season he won twenty-six games, and the season after that, he won twenty-three games, as the Giants captured their third pennant in a row.

It was in the 1912 season when Rube Marquard completely shook off the odious sobriquet of the Eleven-Thousand-Dollar Lemon. During that pennant campaign he achieved his greatest feat as a pitcher, one that went into the record books as a hurling feat of the ages.

Rube Marquard started his winning streak with the very first game the Giants played that season. He pitched the opening game against the Dodgers and, after only six innings of play, Rube Marquard and the Giants had the game stopped because of an impending mob riot. The final score was 18–3, and Rube Marquard had his first victory of that season.

That unique opener launched baseball's most incredible winning streak. Every time Rube pitched thereafter, he won his game. Ten in a row, and still he went on winning. He had fifteen consecutive wins now and fans everywhere wondered how long it would go on. The Rube just kept pitching. He chalked up number 16, then 17, 18, 19 victories in a row. Then on the afternoon of July 8, with the eyes of the whole baseball world on him, the amazing Rube went after his twentieth straight against the Chicago Cubs. But the Cubs not only stopped Rube, they knocked him out of the box to win that game. So ended the longest winning streak by one pitcher in modern baseball history. It stands as a monument to Rube Marquard's pitching skill to this very day!

All in all, Rube Marquard pitched nineteen years in the majors, he won 201 games, and helped his team to win five pennants. But he is only remembered for winning nineteen consecutive games in a single season!

* * *

The first all-salaried baseball team in history was the Cincinnati Red Stockings of 1868. That club had a ten-player payroll of $9300. To justify its worth as baseball's first all-professional team, the Cincinnati Red Stockings didn't lose a game all season, winning sixty-five in a row.

* * *

The greatest accomplishment a major-league batter can achieve is to hit .400 for a full season. In modern major-league history, only seven players have done it. The last time it was performed in the American League was in 1941, when Ted Williams hit 406 and the last time it was accomplished in the National League was in 1930 when Bill Terry hit .401!

It happened only twice in history that one major-league season produced two .400 hitters. In 1911, rookie Joe Jackson of the Cleveland Indians amazed the baseball world by hitting .408! Curiously, in that same season, Ty Cobb of the Detroit Tigers batted .420!

But only once in big-league history a pennant campaign produced three .400 hitters. In 1922, Rogers Hornsby of the St. Louis Cardinals hit .401 to win the National League batting championship. In the American League, Ty Cobb also hit .401 but he did not win the batting title. George Sisler of the St. Louis Browns hit .420!

THE UMPIRE AND THE PICKPOCKET

The major leagues' toughest umpire was George Magerkurth, who had once been a heavyweight prize fighter. Few players were brave enough to tangle with him verbally, while none were foolish enough to tangle with him physically.

However, one day, when big, lumbering George Magerkurth was officiating behind the plate at the once-famed Ebbets Field where the old Brooklyn Dodgers used to play, a little man suddenly climbed out of the stands, strolled onto the playing field, and attacked umpire Magerkurth. Before "Big Mage" knew what had happened, he was stretched flat on his back at home plate, with the little guy astride him, and pummeling him for all he was worth. Police swarmed on the field and hauled the ump's attacker to jail.

The embarrassed George Magerkurth refused to press assault charges against the little fellow who had attacked him and had humiliated him before thousands of baseball fans. When they asked the umpire why he was so willing to forgive and forget, he replied with regal aplomb: "Aw, shucks! That foolish little guy lost his head. I don't want to see him go to jail. I've got a boy of my own."

But later umpire George Magerkurth found out why he had been attacked. In police court the little man confessed that he was a convict out on parole and that he had attacked the major-league ump for purely business reasons. He was a pickpocket by trade and, while he started a rhubarb with the ump, his confederate in the stands could pick pockets during all the excitement on the field.

It took umpire George Magerkurth a long time to get over his double embarrassment—attacked and beaten by a baseball fan half his size, and then discovering that, unknowingly, he had "helped" a pickpocket rob the customers in the ball park who had witnessed his humiliation.

THE GREATEST
PITCHING FEAT DIDN'T COUNT

The major leagues' greatest perfect pitching performance was achieved by Harvey Haddix—but it didn't count for the record book.

On May 26, 1959, a smallish, unimpressive thirty-three-year-old southpaw named Harvey Haddix was sent to the mound to pitch for the Pittsburgh Pirates against the league-leading Milwaukee Braves. He was feeling a little grumpy that day because he was nursing a head cold. He had only one thought in mind as he began to pitch—to end the game as fast as possible. He thought he would be lucky if he could last five innings.

There was no warning on that day in May that an epoch-making performance was under way when little Harvey Haddix began to pitch. But as inning after inning was recorded on the scoreboard, it became evident that a pitching miracle was in the making, and that the small, boyish-looking southpaw was achieving the greatest pitching performance in the history of the major leagues.

At the end of nine innings of play, Harvey Haddix had mowed down twenty-seven batters in a row, to complete a perfect no-hit no-run game.

But strangely, even after retiring twenty-seven batters in a row, Harvey Haddix still hadn't won the game because his teammates had failed to score even a single run for him. So Harvey Haddix's perfect no-hitter went into extra innings. However, the magic of his perfect hurling still kept the miracle going for the awed crowd in the stands. He didn't give up a hit or a walk to any of the batters who faced him in the tenth inning, or in the eleventh, or in the twelfth inning.

It was the greatest pitching feat of all time, but it didn't count. For in the thirteenth inning, the perfect-game miracle suddenly came to an end. An error and a hit lost the game for Harvey Haddix, by a 1–0 score.

THE MOST HATED CLUB OWNER

Andrew Freedman, a New York transportation millionaire, bought the old New York Giants purely for a whim. But no sooner had he become a major-league club owner, than he began to gain a notoriety never before achieved by a big-league club magnate. He abused and quarreled with his own players, brawled with umpires, fought with the league officials, argued with the other club owners, and even battled with the fans who came to watch his team play.

Several times, he barred an umpire from his ball park because the arbiter had dared make a decision which had cost the Giants a game. Once, Andrew Freedman physically attacked a rival club owner, who was so badly beaten he had to be hospitalized.

Andrew Freedman collected enemies by the score. He fired his managers and discarded players on the whim of a moment. Arrogantly, he continued to defy all baseball authority, and too often, he ridiculed and scoffed at the customs and the traditions of the game. By the end of the 1902 season, Andrew Freedman had become so despised and hated as a major-league club owner that he was forced to sell his club and get out of the majors.

However, before he was chased out of baseball, he left his mark on the game with an unforgettable act. In the middle of the 1902 season, against all advice, he had hired a pugnacious, brawling, famous ballplayer to manage his last-place New York Giants. His new pilot was a scrappy troublemaker after his own heart. The little pilot Andrew Freedman had left behind him in the majors remained the Giants' manager for the next thirty consecutive years, and he piloted the Giants to ten pennants. His name was John J. McGraw.

When the cruelest and most hated club owner in major-league history died, he left behind him a legacy to honor his memory—he left all his millions to establish a charity home for millionaires who had lost all their money.

Near the ball park he once had owned, Andrew Freedman's fortune built an institution of luxury where elderly folks of culture and refinement could live during their declining years in the gracious manner to which they once had been accustomed. It is the only charity home in the world where millionaires who went broke can still live in a swanky home, for free—like millionaires.

AN UMPIRE ON ICE

Umpire Bill Stewart not only officiated in the major leagues for twenty-three years, but out of baseball season, he also made hockey history. Once, he managed and coached a big-league pro hockey team and brought it to one of the most astounding triumphs in sports history.

In 1938, he was coaching the Chicago Black Hawks, the most hapless and mediocre club in the National Hockey League. Composed mostly of misfits and cast-offs, Bill Stewart's floundering Black Hawks barely won fourteen games during that entire hockey season. Nevertheless, his team sneaked in by the back door, into the playoffs for the famed Stanley Cup—the "World Series" of hockey.

When the famous big-league baseball umpire predicted that his ludicrous team would capture the Stanley Cup, symbol of the world hockey championship, it became the best joke in the sports world. The odds against such a miracle happening were about a thousand to one.

Nevertheless, spurred on by the baseball umpire who defied the seemingly impossible, Bill Stewart's surprising Black Hawks caught fire, played superbly, and won the treasured Stanley Cup, becoming the hockey champions of the world.

A NEW KIND OF RODEO

Tris Speaker was a star rodeo performer before he achieved glory as the greatest center fielder in major-league history, and a Hall of Fame immortal. Even when the fabulous "Grey Eagle" was the player-manager of

the world champion Cleveland Indians, he still displayed his horsemanship before the baseball fans. On April 21, minutes before game time on the opening day of the 1921 season, he startled more than twenty thousand spectators in the Cleveland ball park by riding a spirited horse.

Although the bucking horse did its wildest best to toss the famous player-manager, nevertheless, with a skilled and firm hand, Tris Speaker subdued the animal and topped off his display of horsemanship with a full-speed gallop around the playing field.

A DEBUT IN JUNE

On the afternoon of June 10, 1944, the St. Louis Cardinals were slaughtering the Cincinnati Reds. At the end of eight innings, the Cards had thirteen runs and the Reds none. In the ninth inning, from the Cincinnati bullpen, came a new relief pitcher. He was a strapping rookie southpaw who had never before pitched in a major-league game. Joe Nuxhall was his name.

The Cincinnati relief pitcher hurled only the ninth inning, for his major-league debut. But it turned into a nightmare for him. Because he gave up five walks and six runs. His one-inning major-league debut left pitcher Joe Nuxhall so flustered and stunned that, as he walked off the mound at the conclusion of the game, he fell flat on his face.

Although Joe Nuxhall's major-league debut was a miserable flop, nevertheless he made baseball history, as the youngest player ever to appear in a major-league game. For on that June afternoon of 1944, relief pitcher Joe Nuxhall was seven weeks shy of his sixteenth birthday!

Curiously, Joe Nuxhall, who began as a relief pitcher in the majors before he was sixteen years old, was still a relief pitcher in the majors, twenty years later.

* * *

A relief pitcher who experienced a more horrifying one-inning major-league debut was Ernie Shore.

On June 20, 1912, the old New York Giants were playing the former Boston Braves. With the Giants far in the lead, relief pitcher Ernie Shore was sent to the mound to hurl the ninth inning. It was his major-league debut as a pitcher. But that single inning turned into a nightmare for him—he gave up eight hits and was clobbered for ten runs.

It was the only inning relief pitcher Ernie Shore ever hurled for the Giants. He was quickly relieved. But five years later Ernie Shore won the most unforgettable game ever pitched by a major-league relief hurler.

On June 23, 1917, the Red Sox played the Washington Senators. The immortal Babe Ruth, then a great left-handed pitcher, started the game for the Red Sox. He walked the first batter, got into a violent argument with the umpire, and was thrown out of the game. So relief pitcher Ernie Shore went to the mound to take over the hurling for the Red Sox.

He took only five warm-up pitches before he began to work in earnest. On his first pitch, the Washington runner attempted to steal, and was thrown out at second. Thereafter, no Senator walked, nor hit, nor reached a base. Twenty-six Senators came to bat, and relief pitcher Ernie Shore retired them all in order. From his first to his last pitch, facing the twenty-six men in a row, he hurled a perfect game!

AN ASSIST FROM BASEBALL

If it hadn't been for baseball, the world might have missed one of its great opera singers.

The pride and joy of first baseman Sid Farrar, who starred with the Philadelphia Phillies for eight years, was his little daughter, Geraldine. Having often brought her to the ball park, Farrar's teammates became so fond of her they adopted her as the team's honorary mascot.

As Sid Farrar's daughter grew older, he discovered she had an unusually fine voice, so he arranged for her to begin professional voice training. However, big-league salaries at the turn of the century were extremely low, and Sid Farrar barely managed his necessary expenses with his meager salary. And music lessons drained the first baseman's income to the limit. He began to wonder how he could raise extra money.

One afternoon after a game, his teammates found him rummaging through the grandstand, collecting all the scrap tin foil he could find. He confessed that he was scrounging for scraps of tin foil so he could sell it to earn a few extra dollars to help pay for Geraldine's voice-training lessons. His teammates decided to help him and Geraldine. And so, after every game, the Philadelphia players scattered through the stands, and searched for scraps of tin foil. All the tin foil collected was then sold by Sid Farrar, and the money paid for voice lessons for his gifted little daughter.

Eventually, the baseball fans learned of Sid Farrar's struggle to give his gifted daughter a musical education, and they decided also to help. As a result, bales of tin foil were delivered to the Phillies' ball park for Sid Farrar to sell. And the happy first baseman made enough money from the sale of the tin foil to send his Geraldine to the finest music teachers.

With that assist from baseball, in time, Sid Farrar's daughter became one of America's finest opera singers. Geraldine Farrar became a beloved prima donna, and her golden voice entertained millions of people.

* * *

George Sisler was one of the greatest players in baseball history. A more picturesque and more graceful first baseman never played in the major leagues. His batting matched his brilliance in the field. Twice he hit over .400 and when an eye affliction impaired his sight and forced him out of the majors after sixteen years of stardom, he left behind him a glittering lifetime batting average of .341 for his fame.

But George Sisler is unique among all the immortals now in baseball's Hall of Fame not for his greatness as a player, but for his blessings as a father. He sent two sons to the big leagues as players—Dick as a first baseman and Dave as a pitcher.

* * *

When Hall of Famer Charles Radbourn made pitching history in the early days of big-league baseball, he was nicknamed "Old Hoss" for a good reason. For he was an incredible hurler with unbelievable endurance. In the eleven seasons he pitched in the National League, he won 308 games.

In the season of 1884, when he was pitching for the old Providence Club, "Old Hoss" Radbourn performed the most amazing hurling feat in all baseball history. In that season, he pitched an astounding total of 745 innings. Of the seventy-two games he hurled that season, he won sixty. Even more unbelievable, he pitched twenty-seven consecutive games, and he won twenty-six in a row. That herculean performance set the all-time winning streak for big-league pitchers, which stands to this day.

YOU NEVER CAN TELL ABOUT A ROOKIE

It was in 1915 when he first popped up in the big leagues. He was a nineteen-year-old boy from Texas, sporting a badger haircut, a shabby carpetbag holding his worldly belongings, and having less than three dollars in his pocket. The St. Louis Cardinals had bought him from a bush-league club, for two hundred dollars. He had been promised a salary of ninety dollars a month, but when the St. Louis club owner saw Rogers Hornsby for the first time, he changed his mind, and offered him only sixty dollars a month to play for the Cardinals. And even at that, he didn't think he had a bargain. Young, unknown Rogers Hornsby was thin as a rail, stood almost six feet tall, and weighed less than 135 pounds. He was a fair infielder, but he looked hopeless at bat.

However, that skinny, weak-looking recruit had so much spirit and ambition that the Cards' manager decided to keep him on for a while. Rogers Hornsby remained in the major leagues for twenty-three years. He became not only one of the greatest second baseman in history, but the greatest right-handed batter of all time.

For Rogers Hornsby there were no detours on the road to big-league fame and fortune. Baseball became his way of life. And as a right-handed hitter of baseballs, he had no equal.

Seven times he won the batting championship of the National League and within a five-season span when he won five batting titles in a row, he gave the most devastating hitting performance ever achieved by a major-league player. During that fantastic hitting spree, he went to bat 2679 times, and hit safely 1078 times— for a batting average of .402! It's a record that has never been equaled.

HE STOLE FIRST BASE

A base-stealer caused a change of baseball rules, and Herman "Germany" Schaefer, the diamond clown, was responsible.

In the early years of this century he was a great third baseman in the majors, starring in the big leagues for fifteen seasons. However, in the legends of the game, he will be remembered always as one of the greatest clowns in baseball history.

Great third baseman and great clown that he was in his time, he also was a great base-stealer, and one act changed the rules.

It happened when he was starring for the Washington Senators. One afternoon they were playing against the Chicago White Sox, and Germany Schaefer, by virtue of a hit, found himself on first. On the next pitch, fleet-footed Schaefer stole second. Impatient, he wanted to steal third, but a teammate was occupying that base. So, on the very next pitch, German Schaefer was in motion again. He startled the White Sox team, and even his own teammates, by running back to first base, and stealing first. It was the strangest "stolen base" ever swiped by a major leaguer. The ball park was stunned with amazement, and the Chicago infield stood as if petrified. Who had ever heard of anyone stealing first base?

Then to the amazement of all, on the very next pitch, Germany Schaefer again stole second. The White Sox players snapped out of their trance and began to yell in protest, as confusion reigned. But the umpire decided that Germany Schaefer was safe on second where he now rightfully belonged, and the official scorer credited him with three stolen bases instead of one.

His stealing of first base created such a controversy in the majors that, to prevent any future "triple-steal" by clowning Schaefer, or anyone else, the lawmakers in baseball wrote into the rule book a new law—no player may steal first base, and, whereas a player may advance on base at will, he may not retreat a base.

* * *

"The Rajah," as he became known, was the only player in National League history to hit .400 or better, three times. In 1924, he batted an awesome .424—the highest batting average in modern major-league history. For his twenty-three years in the majors, the incredible Rajah wound up with a lifetime batting average of .358 and he was enshrined in baseball's Hall of Fame.

THE UNKNOWN PLAYER

One summer many years ago, a college youngster convinced the skeptical manager of the Junction City team, a Class D club in the old Central Kansas League, to hire him as an outfielder. That unknown ballplayer called himself Wilson.

To the pilot's surprise, Wilson proved to be a sure-handed ball hawk in the outfield, a hard hitter at bat, and a speedy runner on the bases. But, after playing in only fourteen games, and although he was slugging at a .355 pace, Wilson suddenly quit, and vanished without an explanation. He was quickly forgotten as a bush-league player.

However, many years later, it was discovered that the once mysterious college boy who had briefly played pro baseball in the old Central Kansas League had become one of the most famous men in the world. He had achieved immortality not only as one of America's greatest generals, but also as the thirty-fourth President of the United States—Dwight "Ike" Eisenhower.

* * *

On July 28, 1875, Joseph E. Borden of the Philadelphia National League club, became the first pitcher in history to hurl a no-hit no-run game. On May 23, 1876, now pitching for the Boston club, he also hurled the second no-hit no-run game in big-league history. But baseball's first no-hit pitcher came to a strange end. Too soon he lost his hurling skill, and he plunged into oblivion so quickly that he finished the 1876 baseball season as the obscure groundskeeper of the Boston ball park.

* * *

The most unforgettable ninety-seven pitches ever made by a major-league hurler for his undying fame were hurled by Don Larsen, on the afternoon of October 8, 1956. For in that major-league game, he faced twenty-seven batters, and he retired all twenty-seven in a row, to become the first and only man to pitch a perfect no-hit no-run game in World Series history.

A SHARP TONGUE
ISN'T ONLY FOR FISHWIVES

Perhaps a manager's sharp tongue is not conducive to the peace and morale of his players, but there have been big-league managers who have used one to score amazing triumphs. And George Stallings had a sharp tongue.

In 1914, he was the manager of a bedraggled and hapless major-league team known as the Boston Braves. That season, his team was fast going nowhere, and on July 4, the mid-point of the major-league pennant race, George Stallings' misfits were buried in last place. A few days later, a dispirited Boston team popped up in a Toronto ball park to play an exhibition game against a

minor-league club. The minor leaguers belted out a whopping victory over the so-called major leaguers, to the tune of 15–2.

When the Boston players returned to their dressing room, manager Stallings was waiting there for them. When they were all assembled, he leaned against the door and laughed. It wasn't a laugh of joy. It was a cold, sneering laugh that cut into the players like a knife.

Then George Stallings' tongue took over. Facing his players, he roared:

"You low-down no-good damn tramps! It's bad enough to trail in your own league but to get your brains knocked out by a minor-league team is too much. You're yellow! Look at yourselves. You call yourselves major-league players. Why I couldn't trade one of you because no one would have you!"

For several minutes the group of men took an unmerciful tongue-lashing from their manager. Stunned by the cruelty of that verbal beating, the players took it in silence, with a cold hatred for the sharp-tongued manager. By the time George Stallings finished his tirade, the players turned into a pack of angry, growling men scratching and fighting for every game. George Stallings' team won thirty-five out of the next thirty-eight games, and, in a smashing surprising finish, the team went from last place to first, to win the 1914 National League pennant.

The day before the first game of the World Series against the powerful Philadelphia Athletics, quoted at odds of 10–1 to win, George Stallings held a meeting with his players, in a hotel room. Suddenly the phone rang. George Stallings answered it, listened for a moment, then began to roar into the phone. Never had the players heard more scorching profanity in all their hard-boiled lives. At last, manager Stallings banged down the receiver and growled at his players: "Can you beat it, men? That was manager Connie Mack I was talking to. He won't let us have his field for practice, he says he doesn't want us to ruin it. He thinks we're just a bunch of semipros. Well, I told him off!"

The climax of that phone drama was that the Boston team went out mad and created a diamond miracle. The Braves won the baseball championship of the world, in a four-game sweep. Only days later did the players discover that the phone call was a hoax, and that George Stallings had arranged with an assistant to phone him so he could make believe that he was tongue-lashing the gentlemanly Connie Mack, just to make his players angry enough to play good ball.

And a manager's vitriolic tongue paid off with rich dividends.

HE PINCH-HIT FOR DEATH

Every spring, a flock of unknown rookies invade the spring training camps, searching for big-league fame and fortune. Few ever crash the majors on their first whirl at the Big Time. But sometimes a rookie is lucky enough to make it big in a hurry, without benefit of a spring training camp. Joseph Wheeler Sewell did because he had to pinch-hit for Death.

It was late in the 1920 pennant campaign, and three teams were running neck-to-neck in pursuit of the American League flag. The Cleveland Indians led the race by only a half-game margin. Meanwhile, buried deep in the obscurity of the low minor leagues was shortstop Joe Sewell, fresh from the Alabama University campus, playing his first season as a baseball pro. He was far away from the big leagues.

But on the afternoon of August 16, 1920, a fast ball thrown by the Yankees' famous submarine pitcher Carl Mays struck the Cleveland Indians' star shortstop Ray Chapman in the head, and within a few hours Chapman was dead. He was the first player to be killed in a major league game.

The shocked Cleveland Indians began a frantic search for a new shortstop. Suddenly, the unknown Joe Sewell, hardly twenty-one years old, and only sixty-six inches tall, was plucked out of obscurity, and brought to the big leagues to star in a grim role—as a pinch-hitter for Death.

Joe Sewell played shortstop for the grief-stricken Indians, in the final twenty-two games of that season, and he filled the spiked shoes of the dead Ray Chapman with heroic splendor. For Joe Sewell not only fielded brilliantly and hit .329, but he also helped the Cleveland Indians win the pennant, and the World Series championship of 1920.

The rookie was to remain in the major leagues for the next thirteen years, play in 1902 big-league games, set an all-time record as a batter for fewer strikeouts in one season, with a mark of four, and amass a lifetime batting average of .312.

TOUCHÉ, MR. JOHNSON

Umpire Henry "Steamboat" Johnson was tough and witty, and always able to defend his dignity. But once he experienced a dreadful loss for words. It happened when that unforgettable ump was assigned to officiate in his first Ladies' Day game.

On that memorable day, when he arrived at the ball park, he was amazed to find it packed to the rafters with a wild crowd of screeching females. When he swaggered out on the field to begin officiating behind home plate, he was startled by his reception. For almost all the women in the stands stood up in a body to jeer at him.

Amused by his hostile reception, Steamboat Johnson walked up close to the stands, boldly faced the hooting mob of shrieking females, silenced them with a courtly

bow, then boomed at them in his most gentlemanly voice:

"Why, girls! I don't think we've been properly introduced."

Whereupon a huge and husky woman leaned over the grandstand rail, broke her parasol over the famous umpire's head, and shrieked with delight:

"Well, we have now, Mr. Johnson!"

* * *

Ignorance is not always bliss.

When Vernon "Lefty" Gomez was pitching for the ever pennant-winning New York Yankees, he was one of the greatest southpaw hurlers in the major leagues. He was also celebrated for his wit.

At the height of his fame, Lefty Gomez courted the beautiful and lovely stage actress June O'Dea. Shortly before he married her, he took her to see her first big-league baseball game. That afternoon, to impress his wife-to-be, Lefty Gomez pitched a tremendous game, but he lost that extra-inning mound duel by a 1–0 score.

After the game, the weary and depressed pitcher was consoled by his sweetheart who sympathetically cooed to him:

"Don't worry, honey! When you pitch tomorrow, you'll win."

"When I pitch tomorrow?" Lefty Gomez exploded in a horrified scream: "Who in hell do you think you're marrying, Iron Man Joe McGinnity?"

THAT'S HOW IMMORTALS ARE MADE

Sandy Koufax never wanted to be a baseball player at all. When he was a high-school boy in Brooklyn, he preferred basketball. He was a promising enough hoop star to gain a basketball scholarship to the University of Cincinnati.

However, because he had played some sandlot baseball, he was persuaded to try out for his college freshman baseball team. Although he was a poor-fielding and weak-hitting first baseman, he nevertheless made the team as a pitcher, because he could throw hard. Then, to Sandy's surprise, he attracted the attention and interest of a scout for the former Brooklyn Dodgers, and was offered a bonus of $20,000 plus a salary of $6,000 a season to pitch in the big leagues.

Sandy was nineteen years old when he came to the major leagues in 1955. Extremely shy, a hopeless wild thrower, and ignorant of pitching techniques, the green rookie managed to win two games in his first season in the big leagues. The following season he was no better as a winning pitcher.

Embarrassed and discouraged, the solemn and proud left-hander wanted to quit baseball. To encourage him to continue as a pitcher, the Dodgers raised his season's salary to $7,000.

In his first six years in the majors, Sandy won only 36 games, while losing 40. But with each victory and defeat, the serious southpaw learned more of the art of pitching. And as the seasons went by, his hurling began to dominate the game.

On August 31, 1959, Sandy, for the first time amazed the baseball world with an unforgettable pitching feat. In a winning night game before 82,794 spectators, he struck out 18 batters in only nine innings. Only once before in modern major league history had such a wondrous strikeout performance been accomplished.

On a sunny afternoon of the following season, Sandy again amazed the baseball world with an incredible strikeout feat. In a winning nine-inning game, he fanned 18 men and became the only pitcher in history to strike out 18 batters in a single game—twice, day and night.

In the 1961 season, the dark and solemnly handsome southpaw won 18 games for the Dodgers, and it seemed that he was on the way to the glory of reaching the plateau of greatness. But early in the 1962 baseball season, after he had twirled his first no-hit no-run game in the majors and won 14 games, Sandy ran afoul of misfortune. Because of a bruise on his left hand, his fingers turned numb and lost their sense of touch. Doctors gloomily told him that he had a rare circulatory ailment. After Sandy was cured, he was told he almost lost a finger on his pitching hand.

In 1963, Sandy astounded the baseball world by staging a remarkable comeback. He not only pitched his second no-hitter in the majors and fanned 306 batters to set a new all-time National League strikeout record, he also won 25 games. His phenomenal hurling won the pennant for the Dodgers, and the World Series championship, too. And in that post-season classic, Sandy set the all-time World Series strikeout record for a single game, by whiffing 15 batters.

Sandy hurled his third no-hitter as a major league pitcher early in the 1964 season. But again he was unlucky. For after he had won 19 games, he injured his left elbow while sliding into a base. It ended his pitching for the balance of that season. Then to his horror, he discovered that he had traumatic arthritis in his left elbow.

With the start of the 1965 major league season, Sandy was resigned to live with his ailment, but remained hopeful of being a once-a-week pitcher for his team. However, once again he amazed the baseball world with wondrous pitching feats. Despite the handicap of his arthritic left arm that had to be packed in ice immediately after every game he pitched, he accomplished one of the most fantastic winning seasons ever achieved by a big-league pitcher.

He twirled a perfect no-hit no-run game to become the only pitcher in history with four no-hitters for his everlasting fame. He completed 27 games, and he won 26. In the 336 innings he hurled, he struck out 382 batters, to set an all-time major league strikeout record for a single season. His incredible pitching not only sparked the Dodgers to another pennant, but in the World Series he hurled two vital shutouts to win the baseball championship of the world for his team.

At the conclusion of his eleventh season in the majors, at the age of 29, the man who had never wanted to be a baseball player, much less a pitcher, had become the most famous hero in the baseball world and the most glamorous and greatest pitcher in the major leagues.

REACH ACROSS THE GENERATIONS

With books that explore disenchantment and discovery, failure and conquest, and seek to bridge the gap between adolescence and adulthood.

☐	PHOEBE Patricia Dizenzo	5524	• $ .75
☐	DAVE'S SONG Robert McKay	5733	• $ .75
☐	I KNOW WHY THE CAGED BIRD SINGS Maya Angelou	5848	• $1.25
☐	TOMBOY Hal Ellson	5983	• $ .75
☐	NOBODY WAVED GOODBYE Elizabeth Haggard	6970	• $ .75
☐	JOY IN THE MORNING Betty Smith	6984	• $1.25
☐	THE BELL JAR Sylvia Plath	7178	• $1.50
☐	I NEVER LOVED YOUR MIND Paul Zindel	7263	• $ .75
☐	THE EFFECT OF GAMMA RAYS ON MAN-IN-THE-MOON MARIGOLDS Paul Zindel	7294	• $ .95
☐	RUN SOFTLY, GO FAST Barbara Wersba	7343	• $ .95
☐	A LONG WAY HOME FROM TROY Donia Whiteley Mills	7530	• $ .75
☐	IT'S NOT THE END OF THE WORLD Judy Blume	7764	• $ .75
☐	THE MAN WITHOUT A FACE Isabelle Holland	7804	• $ .95
☐	THE UPSTAIRS ROOM Johanna Reiss	7818	• $ .95
☐	BONNIE JO, GO HOME Jeanette Eyerly	8030	• $ .95
☐	MY DARLING, MY HAMBURGER Paul Zindel	8172	• $ .95
☐	RICHIE Thomas Thompson	8327	• $1.50

Hey There Sports Fan!

We have something just for you!

- ☐ LIGHTWEIGHT BACKPACKING by Charles Jansen 8355 $1.50
- ☐ GUINNESS SPORTS RECORD BOOK—2nd Ed. by The McWhirters 8058 $1.25
- ☐ BASEBALL'S HALL OF FAME by Robert Smith 7771 $1.25
- ☐ BARTLETT'S WORLD GOLF ENCYCLOPEDIA 7736 $2.25
- ☐ BASKETBALL'S UNFORGETTABLES by Mac Davis 7679 75¢
- ☐ CAUGHT SHORT by Donald Davidson 7654 95¢
- ☐ WINNING TACTICS FOR WEEKEND TENNIS by Trabert & Hyams 7623 $1.95
- ☐ BIKES by Stephen Henkel 7563 $1.25
- ☐ BASKETBALL: GREAT TEAMS, GREAT MEN, GREAT MOMENTS by Allen Camelli 7436 75¢
- ☐ FOOTBALL'S UNFORGETTABLES by Mac Davis 7210 75¢
- ☐ EASY MOTORCYCLE RIDING by Theresa Wallach 6926 95¢
- ☐ SPORT SHORTS by Mac Davis 5851 75¢
- ☐ GREAT MOMENTS IN PRO HOCKEY by Allen Camelli 5572 75¢
- ☐ COMPLETE BOOK OF AUTO RACING by Lyle Engel 5518 95¢
- ☐ BASEBALL'S UNFORGETTABLES by Mac Davis 5354 75¢
- ☐ BASEBALL IS A FUNNY GAME by Joe Garagiola 5286 75¢

Buy them at your local bookstore or use this handy coupon for ordering:

Bantam Books, Inc., Dept. PS, 414 East Golf Road, Des Plaines, Ill. 60016

Please send me the books I have checked above. I am enclosing $_____ (please add 35¢ to cover postage and handling). Send check or money order—no cash or C.O.D.'s. please.

Mr/Mrs/Miss_____

Address_____

City_____State/Zip_____

PS—7/74

Please allow three weeks for delivery. This offer expires 7/75.

START A COLLECTION

With Bantam's fiction anthologies, you can begin almost anywhere. Choose from science fiction, classic literature, modern short stories, mythology, and more—all by both new and established writers in America and around the world.

☐	THE BALLAD OF THE SAD CAFE AND OTHER STORIES Carson McCullers	4216 •	95¢
☐	THE MARTIAN CHRONICLES Ray Bradbury	5613 •	95¢
☐	THE WORLD'S BEST SHORT STORIES Roger B. Goodman, ed.	6502 •	60¢
☐	50 GREAT AMERICAN SHORT STORIES Milton Crane, ed.	6663 •	$1.25
☐	75 SHORT MASTERPIECES: Stories from the World's Literature Roger B. Goodman, ed.	6742 •	95¢
☐	MYTHS AND LEGENDS OF ANCIENT EGYPT T. G. H. James	6824 •	$1.45
☐	MYTHS AND LEGENDS OF ANCIENT GREECE John Pinsent	6827 •	$1.45
☐	THE ALEPH AND OTHER STORIES, 1939-1969 Jorge Luis Borges	7117 •	$1.95
☐	17 FROM EVERYWHERE: Short Stories by World Authors Lee A. Jacobus, ed.	7209 •	95¢
☐	THE NICK ADAMS STORIES Ernest Hemingway	7250 •	$1.75
☐	TEN TIMES BLACK: Stories from the Black Experience Julian Mayfield, ed.	7351 •	95¢
☐	50 GREAT HORROR STORIES John Canning, ed.	7601 •	$1.50
☐	50 GREAT SHORT STORIES Milton Crane, ed.	8192 •	$1.50
☐	WE BE WORD SORCERERS Sonia Sanchez, ed.	8347 •	$1.25
☐	TEN MODERN AMERICAN SHORT STORIES David A. Sohn, ed.	8571 •	95¢
☐	TWENTY GRAND SHORT STORIES Ernestine Taggard, ed.	8609 •	95¢

Buy them at your local bookstore or use this handy coupon for ordering:

Bantam Books, Inc., Dept. EDF, 414 East Golf Road, Des Plaines, Ill. 60016

Please send me the books I have checked above. I am enclosing $_____ (please add 35¢ to cover postage and handling). Send check or money order —no cash or C.O.D.'s please.

Mr/Mrs/Miss_____

Address_____

City_____State/Zip_____

EDF—9/74

Please allow three weeks for delivery. This offer expires 9/75.

FREE!
Bantam Book Catalog

It lists over a thousand money-saving best-sellers originally priced from $3.75 to $15.00 —bestsellers that are yours now for as little as 50¢ to $2.95!

The catalog gives you a great opportunity to build your own private library at huge savings!

So don't delay any longer—send for your catalog TODAY! It's absolutely FREE!